THE
WATER PLANET

Atlantic Ocean, South Coast of La Désirade, Lesser Antilles

THE WATER PLANET

A Celebration of the Wonder of Water

By
Lyall Watson

With Images by
Jerry Derbyshire

CROWN PUBLISHERS, INC.   NEW YORK

Books by Lyall Watson

Supernature
The Romeo Error
Gifts of Unknown Things
Lifetide
Whales of the World
Lightning Bird
Heaven's Breath
Beyond Supernature

Published by Crown Publishers, Inc., 225 Park Avenue South, New York, New York 10003 and represented in Canada by the Canadian MANDA Group.

CROWN is a trademark of Crown Publishers, Inc.

Manufactured in Japan

Library of Congress Cataloging-in-Publication Data
Watson, Lyall.
* The water planet.*
* Bibliography: p.*
* 1. Water—Popular works.   I. Title.*
GB671.W37   1988   551.4   87-6727
ISBN: 0-517-56504-8

Book Design by June Marie Bennett

10 9 8 7 6 5 4 3 2 1

First Edition

CONTENTS

Little Colorado River, Arizona

INTRODUCTION

Water is strange. It is the most abundant liquid in the world. In fact, it is the only inorganic liquid that occurs naturally anywhere on earth. We and our lives are awash with it, and yet it is also highly unusual.

Water is a scientific freak. It has the rare and distinctive property of being denser as a liquid than as a solid, and is the only chemical compound that can be found naturally in solid, liquid, or gaseous states. It is also a powerful reagent, capable in time of dissolving any other substance on the planet. Nothing is safe from it, and yet this unique substance is colorless, odorless, and tasteless. It irrigates all of earth, forming 15 percent of even "dry" dust and covering 71 percent of the globe completely.

Our liquid planet glows like a soft blue sapphire in the otherwise hard-edged darkness of space. There is nothing quite like it in the solar system. There may be nothing to compare with it anywhere in the universe. Water ice has been detected in Saturn's rings and on the nucleus of Halley's comet. There may just be minute quantities of water vapor in the atmosphere of Mars. But not a drop of liquid water has so far been found anywhere else in the galaxy. Nor is there any certain evidence of life out there.

The two seem to be inseparable. We are born of water and need to be sustained by it. It has been so ever since the first living cells, each with its own little reservoir, appeared somewhere in the 326 million cubic miles of water that keep the surface of this planet within very narrow and livable limits.

This then is a portrait, in words and carefully selected images, of less than 3 percent of that total. A look at the small part of the planet's water that is locked up in polar ice caps and glaciers, gathers in lakes both large and small, and flows through the soil and river systems of earth back to an increasingly salty sea.

There is little in this book about the ocean. It is always out there, creating climates, gnawing away at the shore, impossible to ignore. It is part of a water network, a continuous liquid web that holds our lives together. The long ancestral lines of every plant and animal in the world began in the ocean. The sea is our mother, her cadence is part of our unconscious, but there is a very real sense in which salt water is inhuman. It fails in the first duty of water, which is to be sweet and serve us directly, to nourish us.

This, therefore, is a celebration of fresh water. Part prayer in appeasement of the awesome powers of flood and avalanche, but mostly an offering in honor of the cool, fertile spirits of stream and cascade, of fog and soft summer rain. Water is wonderful.

THE
WATER PLANET

Dawn Seascape, Na Pali Coast, Kauai, Hawaii

Part One

WATER AND EARTH

Ice Cave, Glacier Bay National Park, Alaska

*Water may flow in a thousand channels,
but it all returns to the sea.*

AFRICAN PROVERB

2

Sandwood Bay, Sutherland, Scotland

In the beginning, there was no water. Earth was too hot to let it happen. But as the molten core of the planet slowly settled, producing a viscous mantle and a thin outer crust, it covered itself in a dense cloud of methane, ammonia, and carbon monoxide. In time, this poisonous, early envelope boiled off into space and a new atmosphere began to develop—one dominated by hydrogen and carbon dioxide and, eventually, by water vapor.

Then it rained.

At first the water steamed and swirled high above the heated surface, but eventually the crust cooled sufficiently to allow vapor to condense and, for millions of years, through the longest, darkest night of our world's existence, the rains came down.

Composite: Iona Seascape, Scotland/Isla Mujeres Thunderstorm, Mexico

Drops of water thickened and formed in the upper atmosphere, growing large enough to fall on a warm surface that shot fresh clouds of vapor directly back into the air, feeding an endless deluge. And the giant storm continued until earth was battered and eroded and liquid came to rest in every hollow—and darkness lay upon the face of the deep.

When the dense clouds lifted and sunlight succeeded in breaking through, it fell, not on a brash new land, but on carved peaks rising from the first seas. These were virtually fresh seas with just a trace of dissolved mineral salts picked up by water busy changing the face of the planet.

4

North Sea, Faraid Head, Sutherland, Scotland

Lower Falls of the Yellowstone River, Wyoming

In effect, every raindrop is a bullet, taking the shape of an almost perfect sphere, whose surface tension makes it tough enough to blast microscopic bits out of any landscape. And as drops and their debris gather, they form abrasive trickles that continue carving up a surface, growing quickly in both power and momentum, until they become torrents which roar down a mountainside, shattering and grinding any rocks that may stand in their way.

Pfeiffer, Big Sur, California

This is how erosion takes place. How stone becomes sculpted and soil is made. Left to itself, the process would eventually lead to a planet with a smooth face, covered by an unbroken ocean over two miles deep everywhere. But the wearing down is balanced by a building up, by the growth of new mountains in place of old. And the result is a complex and wonderfully weathered landscape, no longer without form and void, set in an ever more salty sea.

This bald, almost mythical, account of earth's creation makes it sound inevitable. It wasn't. For water to exist at all, in any form, there had to be a set of cosmic coincidences so inherently unlikely that they are hard to distinguish from miracles of design.

Water cannot come to be without hydrogen and, by all the laws of physics, there should be none of that gas left on earth. Hydrogen is the lightest of all elements and a planet of our size simply doesn't have enough gravity to hold on to it. Most hydrogen has, in fact, escaped into space. But just enough, around 1 percent, was captured and condensed and held in combination with other heavier elements, such as carbon and silicon and sulfur. And it stayed there until the planet had cooled to a point where it was exactly the right density and size to hold on to free hydrogen seeping from the rocks of the crust—as long as each pair of such fleeting atoms was anchored to a single, heavier atom of oxygen, as water.

9

Esplanade, Surprise Canyon, Grand Canyon National Park, Arizona

Summit of Soufrière, Guadeloupe, Lesser Antilles

And the coincidences don't end there. To keep wet, earth had not only to be the right size, but had to fall into orbit at precisely the right distance from our particular sun.

Temperatures in the universe range from the deep freeze of space to the thermonuclear heat of blazing stars. Within this immense span of over thirty-six million degrees, fluid water can occur only within the narrow band of 180 degrees Fahrenheit that lies between its freezing and its boiling points. And for reasons that remain difficult to explain, our planet is just far enough from a star of exactly the right size and condition to prolong what ought to be a rare and fleeting instant on the temperature scale into four billion years of liquid history.

Today our planet is bathed in 326 million cubic miles of water. Enough, if earth is reduced to the size of a schoolroom globe, to make its surface only just damp to the touch. But sufficient, given its actual size, to create a delicate and paradoxical membrane that shifts and swirls about our world, giving it a soft and very special quality. An endowment likely to catch and hold the attention of any cosmic observer, who couldn't fail to stop and look, and see, and say they saw that it was good. It is good. And it is water that keeps it so.

Our sun is an uncontrolled radiant heater with an erratic output. Like all other stars of the main sequence, it is in the throes of its own violent evolution, and now gives out three times as much energy as it did when earth was young four billion years ago. But our planet is not now three times as hot as it was then. It is water-cooled. The surface stays within the same astonishingly narrow limits largely because every square foot of it enjoys the soothing balm of roughly forty thousand gallons of water in some form.

13

Tidal Pools, Hanakahau, Kona, Hawaii

Seascape, Aird Fenish, Isle of Lewis, Scotland

The total quantity of water on earth has remained constant during most of our history, but it has never, of course, been equally distributed.

Ever since the first great rains, the vast majority of our water supply has gathered aboveground in the ocean basins. About 317 million cubic miles, or 97.2 percent of all water, is still there. But it is never still.

In theory, there is a direct attraction between every drop of sea water and even the most distant star in the universe. Gravity ties all matter together in an infinite and vibrant web. But in practice, it is only our local star, the sun, and our natural satellite, the moon, that exert any overt influence. Working, sometimes in concert and sometimes in opposition, to create the ebb and flow of the tides.

15

The lunar effect is the strongest, tugging insistently at water on earth's surface, pulling it away from the body of the planet like a loose garment. Whole oceans flow out toward the moon, bringing high tide to any land that happens to lie in that direction; and doing so again the next day, precisely forty-eight minutes later.

Twice a month, when the moon is full and when it appears as just a thin, silver thread, sun and moon and earth all fall directly into line, and this joint attraction of our two nearest neighbors carries the ocean up to the brim of every creek and dock on the highest of tides, the ones we call springs.

At other times, most notably at the quarters of the moon, when sun and moon and earth lie at the points of a triangle, lunar and solar influences almost cancel each other out. But even then, every drop of water in the world still responds to cosmic call, and infinitesimal neap tides can be measured in pools as isolated and confined as a cup of tea.

Every area of water, each gulf and arm of every sea, has its own tidal character, its own natural frequency and period of oscillation. All are subject to regional vagaries, to swirls and overfalls, to rips and bores that elaborate on the underlying rhythms. The result is confusion so profound that it can only be controlled by computer-generated tide tables. And even then these need to be used with caution and interpreted by those who have lived long enough to have intimate local knowledge.

17

Moonrise, Pointe des Châteaux, Guadeloupe, Lesser Antilles

There are other, more general, influences on earth and water.

Because of the angle at which the sun's rays strike our atmosphere, and the distance radiation has to travel to reach the surface, there is an unequal distribution of solar heat. Polar air and seas are always colder than those on the equator. But the disequilibrium is made much less severe by the existence of great planetary currents.

These begin with air that warms and rises over the equator and has its place taken by trade winds, which blow diagonally in from the cooler midlatitudes, pushing all surface waters westward until they bounce off the nearest continent and set up huge circular eddies that turn clockwise in the northern and counterclockwise in the southern hemisphere.

The result of such wholesale circulation of water is a massive redistribution of heat energy. Where an ocean current is just ten degrees warmer than the land it touches, every cubic mile delivers as much heat as would normally be generated by burning five million tons of coal. And great ocean rivers like the Gulf Stream, which carry three million cubic miles of warm water up to the cool shores of the north Atlantic every hour, bring more warmth to those high latitudes in that hour than could be provided by burning all the coal mined everywhere in the world for a year.

Juan Perez Sound, Queen Charlotte Islands, British Columbia

This kind of heating is direct and effective, bringing tropical plants into flower in southwestern Ireland. But it is cumbersome, a little like taking a hot water bottle to bed. There are more subtle methods of climatic control that involve central air-conditioning.

These begin in the same way, with heat beating down on a tropical ocean. Water temperatures rise and some of the sea evaporates, carrying with it a quantity of heat energy locked in its molecules. This warm water vapor is lifted into the upper atmosphere and carried near the ceiling toward the poles, where much of it is chilled and falls as snow. And as it changes from vapor to solid, it releases the heat it picked up near the equator, raising the temperature of the air over Greenland or Antarctica.

Heat exchange of this kind is not confined to polar regions. Evaporation from the surface of the sea goes on all the time, fast enough to drain the ocean reservoir completely once every three thousand years. Water vapor fuels all the winds of the world with around twelve thousand cubic miles of liquid every year, producing huge and largely invisible rivers that flow through the air at every level, sharing out energy and information, distributing warmth and awareness, bringing water and life to the land.

Seascape, Pointe des Châteaux, Guadeloupe, Lesser Antilles

22

Cumshewa Inlet, Queen Charlotte Islands, British Columbia

If such quantities are hard to comprehend, it is worth bearing in mind that a cubic mile of water contains over a billion gallons. Enough to fill forty million swimming pools, or to bathe everyone on earth five times over.

The aerial component of the world's water resources may form only 0.001 percent of the total at any one time, but it is the source of over six million cubic miles of water now locked up in ice caps and glaciers. Through rain and snow, it supplies the world's lakes and rivers directly with the fifty-five thousand cubic miles of water they currently contain. And, more important, it is the main source of replenishment for almost two million cubic miles of groundwater that feeds the springs and wells of the world.

These quantities may sound large, but the hard truth of it is that, with over 97 percent of the world's water in the sea and another 2 percent in deep freeze, there is comparatively little left over for daily use. Our planet is a great place for whales and penguins, but evidently not an easy one on which to earn a terrestrial living.

Muir Glacier, Glacier Bay National Park, Alaska

There was a time, not that long ago, when even scientists believed that the water found in rivers came directly from the center of the earth. It was not until the late seventeenth century that Edmund Halley, he of the comet, did some simple arithmetic. He calculated the amount of water flowing from all the rivers of Europe and North Africa into the Mediterranean. He found that the combined flow was roughly equal to the quantity of water falling as rain or snow on that whole drainage area. He seems to have been the first to become aware of the cycle in which water goes from earth to sea to atmosphere and back to earth again.

Halley went on to work out the mechanics of the monsoon, but he was a man well in advance of his time. It was not until over a century later that meteorology was put on a truly scientific basis with the first proper classification of clouds.

Air is normally invisible, even with water vapor in it. But as it expands and cools, it reaches dew point and the vapor condenses into minute droplets. These are light enough to remain airborne, suspended by the swirl of other particles. Fifty billion of them would scarcely fill a teacup, and yet it is these tiny tears that supply the pigment with which winds paint great diagrams of atmospheric flow across the sky. They are the substance of clouds, liquid air rendered locally visible by a fall in temperature.

It is easy, when dealing with clouds in casual glimpses, to think of them as objects in the air. They are not. They are part of the air itself and do not fall because they have never risen. Clouds are simply parts of that thin fluid we call air, parts in ceaseless motion, being constantly renewed. Cascades of water in the air, arrested by the eye in midmovement. Caught from fleeting time by our minds, or given a lasting and sober existence on canvas by painters like John Constable.

Lipan Point, Grand Canyon National Park, Arizona

Composite: Isle of Rhum, Scotland/Bass Trailhead, Grand Canyon, Arizona

Clouds were once the thrones of gods, or seen as symbols of airy grace and dark transgression. But in 1803, an amateur naturalist in England brought them down to earth. Luke Howard invented names for the major forms—drawing on Latin for *cumulus*, meaning "a heap or pile," for the common fairweather forms; *stratus*, meaning "a spread or layer," for the ones stretched out like blankets against the light; and *cirrus*, meaning "a cord or tuft," for the most wispy filaments of the upper sky.

Cloudscape, Caravelle Beach, Guadeloupe, Lesser Antilles

Howard qualified these generic titles with the specific terms *nimbus,* for those bearing rain; and *alto,* for the higher varieties. And with this small but inventive vocabulary, he was able to describe all the panoply of cloud effects and create an excellent natural taxonomy, based on both structure and behavior, that now recognizes twenty-six species of cloud.

Cirrus is the largest genus. The elite among clouds, cool and lofty, nothing but silver lining. These are the eyelashes of the sun, visible from two hundred miles away, holding the warm colors of the day long after the lower clouds have all gone gray. Their substance is diffuse, consisting largely of snowflakes that form over six miles high and grow as they fall, cascading down through the upper levels of the atmosphere. They are whipped by the wind into long streaks of icy spume, woven into fibers with frayed edges, or fluffed up into tufts and turrets.

Closely related to these wing-feathers of the wind are two slightly more earthy genera. *Cirrocumulus,* composed of regular wave patterns of ice grains laid down on the leading edge of a warm front; and *cirrostratus,* the milk cloud, a high and silky veil of crystal that throws a halo round the sun.

Cloudscape, Mount Rodgers, Virginia

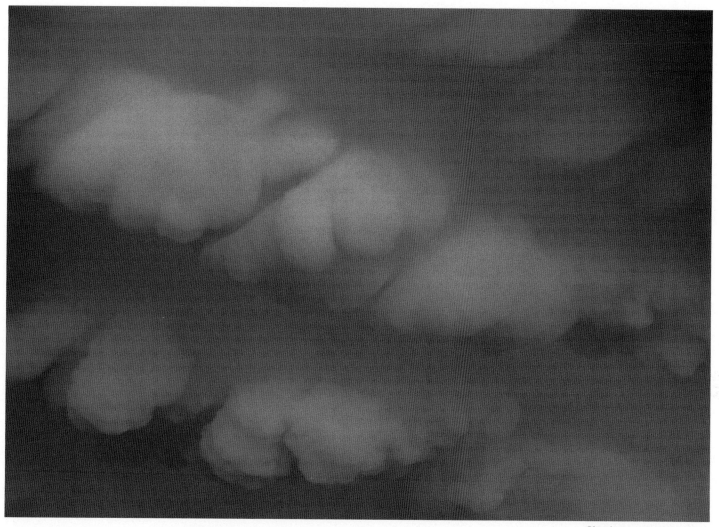

Cloudscape, Austin, Texas

Closer to the ground are the wet blankets of the heavens. Uppermost of these is usually *altostratus*, thin enough to just let the sun shine through, as if it were being seen through ground glass. Beneath this lie the continuous canopies of *stratocumulus*, like somber, partly folded, canvas awnings. And under them all is the shapeless, homespun substance of *stratus*, the most stable of clouds, always a dour blue-gray, touching the ground as a dismal drizzle.

The blanket clouds are stolid, but they, and sometimes even the airy upper forms, are disturbed by far more dynamic species, the radicals of the family.

Unlike all the others, *cumulus* are vertical clouds, puffs of steam generated by hot, rising air, the caps on winds that blow straight up from bare ground or rocky slopes and hills. They usually appear in the middle of a sunny morning, springing up all at the same altitude, like fluffy cabbages in a field of summer sky. Sometimes they gather along the shore in the way of sheep grazing together at a fence line, marking out the margin of the land. Always they roll and grow and change, bursting with evolutionary vigor; upwardly mobile clouds which, given enough moisture, can rise to the top of their procession and become the rampant superstructures we know as *cumulonimbus*—mature and towering thunderheads.

At any one time, roughly 50 percent of earth is covered in some type of cloud as 340 cubic miles of water a day is evaporated from land and ocean surfaces. And every day, exactly the same quantity falls back to earth, 70 cubic miles of it returning to the land as dew, frost, fog, rain, hail, or snow.

Cumulus, Na Pali, Kauai, Hawaii

Dew is a special form of precipitation, a kind of rain conjured from a clear sky. It comes as a gentle benediction, drawn from the vapors of the night, softening the start of a hot summer day. After sundown, soil and sea hold warmth relatively well, but plants radiate their heat rapidly back into space. And if the night is cloudless, lacking a blanket to conserve the day's energies, that radiation soon makes them cooler than the surrounding air. Cool enough to condense their water vapor into tiny, pearly globules of dew.

Such droplets cling to leaf and cobweb, decorating every spear of grass with a sparkling bead, drenching shoes more thoroughly than rain, whose drops are heavier and soon run through to the ground.

Kokee State Park, Kauai, Hawaii

In the tropics, where air is warm and may hold up to ten times as much moisture as it does in temperate areas, the dense canopy of a rain forest radiates heat so fast that dew gathers and falls in heavy showers to the ground. But even in the deserts of the world, where skies are invariably clear, the quantity of dew can be substantial—the equivalent of up to fifteen inches of rainfall every year.

In the Negev, in Sonora and Atacama, there are quantities of smooth pebbles, gathered into mounds as if the surrounding desert fields had been neatly cleared of stones. These attract dew like magnets, condensing moisture out of the air in the early mornings and conserving it from evaporation later in the day. The precious liquid seeps through the piles to moisten earth at the base of a tree or is channeled by lines of such stones into great rock cisterns, many of them lying otherwise inexplicably at the tops, rather than the bottoms, of mountains. Making it possible for a desert people with such dew ponds to support greater populations than any of us can in these areas today, even with all our technology.

Where altitude or latitude is high, radiation on a clear night can bring temperatures well below the freezing point. Then moisture forms, not as dew, but as the icy filigree of a hoar frost, which can be spectacular. Trees and shrubs are transfigured, decorated with bewitching nets of crystal, festooned with frozen lace. Housetops are garlanded in ice too fine to fall and even barbed wire fences sparkle like tiaras. Until the day warms and all this fancy finery just melts away.

37

Roan Mountain, Appalachian Trail, Tennessee

Sawtooth Lake, Idaho

Strath Dionard, Sutherland, Scotland

Clouds, on the whole, are apt to form well above our heads. But not always. Sometimes they cling to earth as mist or fog.

When moist air is cooled by radiation from the ground, or by being carried across cold water, or when vapor rises from warm water into cooler air, it soon reaches saturation point. Spherical droplets form, each denser than air, but so small that eight thousand can accumulate in a single cubic inch. In totally calm air, these little globules fall to earth or become entangled in spiders' webs; and in a wind, they soon get swept away. But when the air is just buoyant enough, the droplets lift and swirl and gather into clouds that hug the ground, dripping moisture on every object in their way. Or, if the air is cold enough, depositing it on smoother surfaces as a shroud of frozen rime.

Such fog-filled air is heavy, draining downhill to accumulate in river valleys, spilling through mountain passes to lie thickly on the coastal plains, or lurking along the western coasts of continents in low-lying banks with astonishingly sharp edges. Fogs have walls and seem to be confined by cliffs of cold, by rigid margins that determine where they can or cannot be.

Most grounded clouds are thickest around sunrise, when humidity is highest, and dissipate soon after dawn. But many are dense enough to reflect sunlight and resist dispersal until well into the day. Then airports close, traffic piles up on the freeways, and shipping creeps along the coast, dead slow ahead and radar at the ready. And when cold clouds get trapped below warmer, drier air aloft, creating an inversion over a city, pollution adds to the problem and foments the poisonous accumulation of a smog.

No clouds are peaceful places. All are overloaded, poised on the brink of energetic disaster, rendered inherently unstable by the fact that each supports thousands, often millions, of tons of water, every drop eight hundred times heavier than air. Sooner or later this water has to fall, most often as rain.

Cloud crises and resulting rain are usually precipitated by cooling. Rising air lifts cumulus clouds, cooling them by five degrees for every thousand feet upward they travel, condensing water vapor into the large drops characteristic of afternoon and evening showers in most warm climates. These are convection rains.

Kalalau Valley, Kauai, Hawaii

42

Loch Scridain, Isle of Mull, Scotland

In temperate areas, rainfall is more often frontal, brought on when heavier, cooler masses of air force their way in under warm ones with lots of water vapor. The slope of such a cold front is usually oblique, and cooling and expansion are gradual, producing condensation that is general and may continue for days. These are convergent rains.

Both kinds of crisis are modified by local conditions, which means that rain, however it is produced, is distributed very unequally over the earth.

In polar areas, the air is too cold to retain much water vapor. The same is true of coasts at all latitudes paralleled by cold ocean currents. And humidity is always low in the deep interior of large continents or behind coastal ranges that milk incoming winds of most of their oceanic moisture.

The average stay of any water molecule in the air is about ten days and most of the 120 thousand cubic miles of rain that falls each year does so in cloud bursts over tropical forests. More than half of it ends up in the Amazon. The highest recorded rainfall anywhere showers down at the rate of over a thousand inches a year on fabled Cherrapunji in the hills of Assam. And the island of Reunion in the southern Indian Ocean is regularly drenched by torrents of up to seventy inches in a single day. Even Unionville in Maryland was once inundated by over an inch of water in a minute.

Rain that heavy is hard to imagine. It no longer falls in discrete drops, but in strings of water forming opaque curtains so dense that buckets of it can be scooped up and drunk directly from the surface of the sea.

Palisades of the Desert, Grand Canyon, Arizona

Very often such storms are preceded by a cooler and still more solid herald, by a fall of frozen rain or hail. Strangely enough, to have hail, there must be heat. Hail seldom occurs in the winter, but owes its origin to updrafts that breed in the great convection storms of summer, carrying drops of water rapidly up to forty thousand feet, where they freeze. And, having frozen, fall. And as they fall, sweep up drops of water in their path, growing as they go.

Most hailstones are small and conical, shaped like a space capsule designed for easy reentry into the atmosphere. But the larger ones, which have ridden the elevator of air in a cloud as often as twenty-five times, tend to be irregular, sometimes even lobed. The largest ever recorded was six inches in diameter, weighing almost two pounds, and fell on Coffeyville in Kansas. All stones of every size are intricate structures, with complex fossil forms of concentric light and dark layers of ice, from which their brief histories, and that of the storm which spawned them, can be read.

Snow is an altogether different matter. It does not depend on any kind of rain, and its creation is a matter of miraculous and infinite variety.

Snow begins in a winter cloud, with relatively warm, moist air rising in an updraft until the vapor in it freezes into hexagonal crystals of ice. Millions of these icy seeds swarm through the air, slowing as they grow, picking up extra water molecules that attach themselves to the lattice, adding to its sixfold symmetry.

The result is a delicate branching form, a flower of the sky, airy architecture that grows still further as it falls, emerging from the base of the cloud bristling with spangles of rime. Something like a trillion such crystal blooms fall from a single snowstorm, and every single one is different. It has been calculated that the weight of snow fallen since earth began may amount to fifty times the mass of the planet, containing a total of 10^{35} crystals. An unimaginably large number, and yet, given the complexity of snow crystal structure, and the fact that each contains some 10^{18} molecules of water, it seems possible that there may never have been two that are exactly alike.

Gila Wilderness, New Mexico

45

As a rule, these filigrees of aerial ice seldom descend singly. They come floating down in bunches that we call snowflakes. And these fall like feathers, piling up one upon another until they look, very properly, snow white. Snow isn't actually white at all. It is, of course, just water and therefore colorless, but the play of light on the molecules of ice, the reflection and refraction from a million crystal surfaces, is almost blinding and produces the effect we expect.

Snowscape, Marion County, Oregon

Watching snowflakes fall is like seeing smoke take form. Each is so delicate, so nearly weightless that it can sit almost unnoticed on an eyelash. It alights so gently, balancing with such precision, that impossible towers grow even on threads of gossamer. There is so much air trapped in and between flakes that a fall becomes an eiderdown, a white blanket insulating soil and plants, imposing silence on the land, making it possible for animals and humans to stay warm and to breathe even when trapped deep beneath such a drift.

49

Alpenglow, Alaska Range, Denali National Park, Alaska

50

Denali, Alaska

And yet, as flakes accumulate, they can become very weighty. Roofs collapse under the growing mass, and trees splinter and crack unless their leaves or branches are specifically designed from time to time to shed the growing load. Even mountains creak and groan beneath their burdens, letting fields of snow cling to the surface until something as slight as the footfall of a rabbit, a sort of "hare trigger," sends thousands of tons thundering down into the valleys, sweeping up everything in its path, blasting even those beyond its reach with great gouts of compressed air, leaving entire landscapes in smoking ruin.

In all these ways, from gentle dew to brutal avalanche, water is brought whispering or roaring back to earth. Every day seventy cubic miles of it settles somewhere on the surface, moistening, cooling, warming, cleansing, and irrigating the land.

Not all of it, however, is readily available for use. Over the centuries, a total of over six million cubic miles has been trapped in ice caps, enough to nourish all the rivers of the world for a millennium, but eked out only gradually, inch by inch, by glaciation.

53

Fairweather Range, Glacier Bay National Park, Alaska

Six million square miles, or 12 percent of the land surface, is permanently covered in ice. It was not always so.

Starting about thirty-five million years ago, there was a general and gradual cooling of the earth. Arguments still rage about the causes—changes in solar radiation or the tilt of the planet are most often mentioned—but it seems certain that ten million years ago, this cooling had gone far enough to produce permanent snows in Antarctica and Greenland.

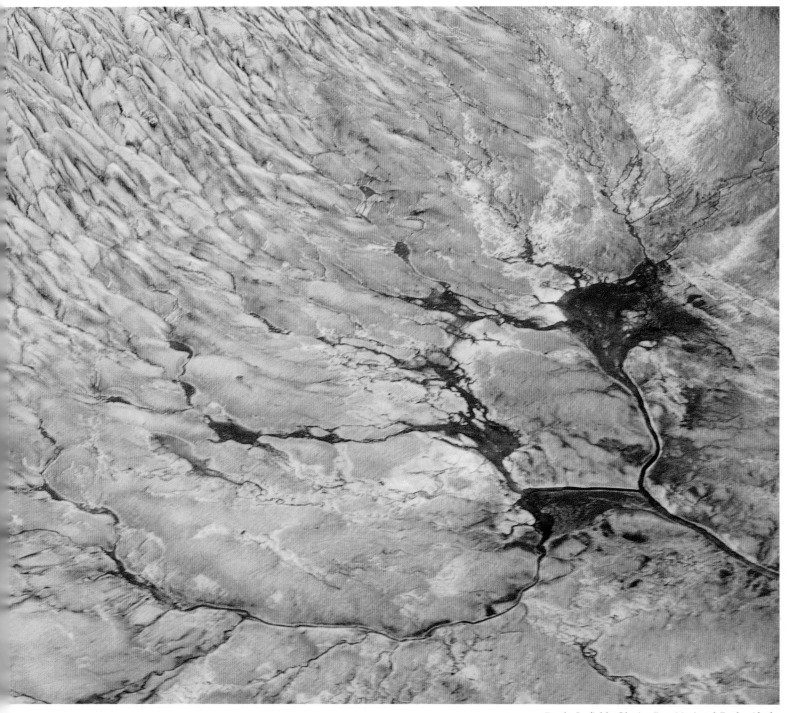

55

Brady Icefield, Glacier Bay National Park, Alaska

When snow is deep enough and lies long enough to lose some of its air under pressure, it becomes bluer in color and more and more transparent. This is *firn*, and if it persists for more than a single season, it grows and grows in density, until ten inches of it packs into one inch of granular ice. By two or three million years ago, such ice had come to cover the earth in gigantic fields, becoming solidly established in the world's first glaciers as we went through a period of unusually severe weather—a time that has come to be known as the first Ice Age.

Ice Cave, Glacier Bay National Park, Alaska

Riggs Glacier, Muir Inlet, Glacier Bay, Alaska

There have been others since, four it seems in all, each lasting around one hundred thousand years, during which ice accumulated at the poles and on the higher plateaus. Some of it simply grew until, in places, it was over a mile deep, weighing down the land, compressing the earth's crust with burdens from which it continues to rebound. Areas in Sweden are still rising in relief at a rate of half an inch a year. But other parts of the great ice caps also started to flow, changing from static blocks to frozen rivers that spread out over the world, creeping down valleys and into warmer lands.

It seems so patently absurd that a substance as brittle as glass should flow like treacle down a slope too shallow to dislodge snow, that it is only a century since scientists ceased to deny that it would happen at all. It certainly does. Glaciers travel, faster in the center than at the sides, at up to eighty feet a day. The gigantic tongues of ice that slip from central Greenland to the sea cover over five miles a year. They flow, as liquids will, swinging wide round bends in a valley, accepting tributaries, breaking up into turbulent lumps on steeper sections, splitting and healing, sometimes even losing all cohesion as they go tumbling over cliffs as frozen waterfalls.

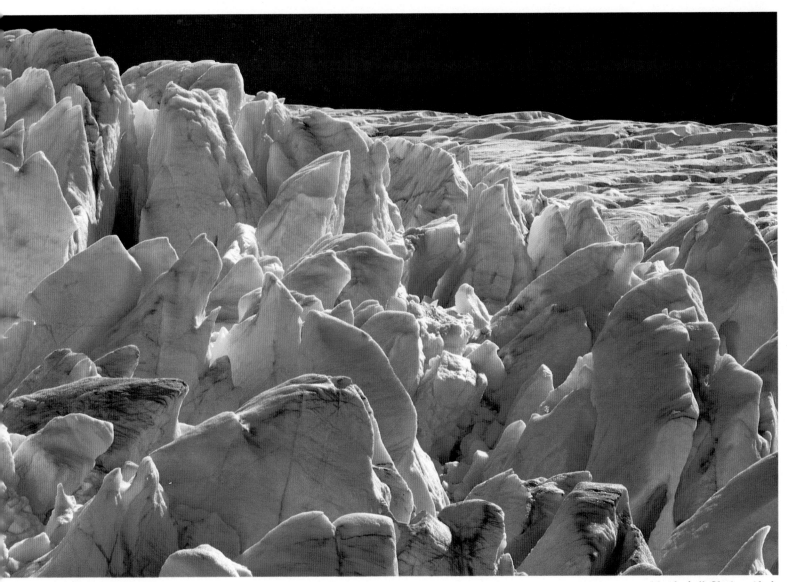

Mendenhall Glacier, Alaska

Ice may be plastic enough to behave in this way, but it is also cohesive enough to leap barriers, to pluck up boulders in its path and drag concentrations of these like a rasp across the land, polishing the substrate, and turning everything else into a fine rock flour. Slopes are gouged into steep U-shaped troughs, leaving tributary valleys hanging high above the floor. Spurs and ridges are ironed out, and all the particularly hard bits are carted off to distant places and dumped there in clusters called knobs and kettles, or in ridge-like moraines.

Next to convulsions in the planet's crust, ice has done more to change the face of earth than any other agency. It has reversed the course of rivers, created and destroyed great lakes, changed the direction of evolution, and shifted the boundaries between land and sea.

When glaciers run directly into the sea before melting, they calve. Great chunks break away along a frontal cliff and crash down into the water of fjords, turning end over end until they reach equilibrium, throwing up tidal waves that batter the shore. Greenland gives birth each year to over ten thousand such iceberg offspring that sail off to the south, creating panic in the shipping lanes until they melt and die two years later.

In the Antarctic, a floating crust of barrier ice extends far out to sea where the margin is eroded until monstrous, tabular bergs are detached. These floating mountains, rising fifteen hundred feet from the sea, may be thirty or forty miles long and live on for ten years or more, drifting through the southern seas like ghostly cities of alabaster and marble.

61

Lamplugh Glacier, Glacier Bay National Park, Alaska

Kinder Downfall, Derbyshire, England

Landlocked glaciers send their water back to the sea in more leisurely fashion, through the river system that drains 70 percent of our surface.

These arteries of earth, which begin in capillary creeks, streams, brooks, and rivulets, are in the transport business. They carry thirty-four thousand cubic miles of water back each year to its home in the sea, along with some sixteen billion tons of freight in the form of topsoil and sediment. Rivers do not necessarily always have water in them. Some are no more than seasonal, arroyos. But it is characteristic of all rivers, no matter what their size, that they move in only one direction—downhill. It is gravity that drives a river's search for the sea.

Colorado River, Granite Gorge, Grand Canyon, Arizona

Mississippi River, Grand Gulf, Mississippi

Some never find it, falling into holes in the ground and disappearing forever. Others get lost and give up in thirsty desert sands. But most make the journey successfully, closing the cycle that starts with evaporation and the temporary loan of large quantities of water from the surface of the sea.

The majority of rivers begin their active lives as minor streams occupying some incidental irregularity near a coastline. And as they grow, they compete for resources, seeking tribute from other areas of drainage, digging deeper channels, pushing their heads back farther and farther inland. They capture and divert competitors and enlarge their flow, gradually establishing dominance over bigger and bigger basins. Until perhaps they get to be as mighty as the Amazon, which stretches back four thousand miles, is fed by a thousand tributaries, many big enough to be considered as major rivers in their own right, and drains an area the size of the face of the moon.

Rivers are powerful shapers of land. They level mountains, cut enormous canyons like that of the Colorado, which lies now more than a mile deep, dwarfing the river itself with walls that tell of two billion years of history.

Grand Canyon from Hance Mine, Arizona

Grand Canyon from Yavapai Point, Arizona

Sometimes rivers make mountains, leaving pillars of harder rock in dramatic isolation as they go about their business of making soil, taking delight in hurling it into the sea where it settles again to become the seed of future continents.

The Mississippi moves a million tons of solid matter a day, dropping some of it in levees on the way. It and the Ganges and the Yangtze and the Nile are all busy building new coastlines, pushing their silted deltas ever deeper out to sea, growing grass where ships once safely moored. Thanks to the alluvial efforts of the Euphrates, the ancient port of Babylon now lies four hundred miles inland.

Mississippi River Delta, Louisiana

Some great rivers like the Amazon, which flows at a speed of six knots and discharges over three million cubic feet a second, are surprisingly flat. From the border of Peru, two thousand miles from the mouth, it falls less than three hundred feet—a drop of not much more than an inch in every mile. Younger rivers tend to be less easygoing, busy still with ambitious schemes, hurling themselves at obstacles and leaping over cliffs.

Elves Chasm, Grand Canyon National Park, Arizona

Whenever there are abrupt changes in geology, there will be rapids, cataracts, and waterfalls. Niagara Falls stands where water passes from a bed of hard limestone to one of soft and more easily quarried shale. Victoria Falls exists because of a rift in the basaltic bed of an otherwise peaceful Zambezi River. In time, both will cease their turmoil as water does its work of denudation, carving up and leveling out the land.

Where barriers stand beyond depressions in the surface, rivers often pause and reflect, taking on the placid character of lakes. There is more than fifty-four thousand cubic miles of water hanging about in this way right now, a volume one hundred times greater than that which actually flows in all the rivers of the world combined. Most of it is held in only brief abeyance, feeding rivers that resume at an outlet. But 45 percent lies in dead-end lakes that have no overflow and gradually turn into salty, inland seas, some of them well below the level of the ocean.

Midway Lake, Alaska

And that is by no means all. Roughly three feet of water falls each year on every square foot of land. Six inches of this goes more or less directly back into the sea. Two further feet are lost to evaporation. And the remaining six inches seeps into the soil, filling every interstice, each cavity and hollow, like a sponge. These are earth's reserves, subterranean stores of liquid treasure—1,680,000 cubic miles of it. Enough, if taken up and spread out over the surface, to cover all land to a depth of one thousand feet.

This is groundwater. A sea beneath our feet. A gigantic reservoir that feeds all the natural springs and fountains of earth. Some of it bubbles up in cool, green eyes; and some, having sunk too deep, bursts back into the light in steam and riot, as geysers or thermal springs, often fouled with sulfur

fumes.

Blue Spring, Little Colorado River Gorge, Arizona

Much of the rest lies just beneath the surface and can be reached by driving a well or borehole down to the level of the water table, bleeding the veins of earth itself. There is no harm in this, at least in moderation. Some of the world's great civilizations have flourished as a direct result of such skills in arid areas. But there are now perhaps ten million wells in the United States alone, and it will not be long before we drain some organs in the body of the planet completely dry. And there is peril, and a certain sacrilege, in that.

Taken all in all, the ocean, the atmosphere, and the aquifers of earth form a single and colossal circulatory system. A network directly responsible for temperature and humidity control. A system that keeps the planetary organism nourished and informed, alive and well beneath the shelter and protection of its thin liquid skin. Without water, life would be impossible.

75

Lingo's Well, Coshocton, Ohio

Minnie's Run, Okefenokee Swamp, Georgia

Part Two

WATER AND LIFE

Cypress Tree, Atchafalaya Swamp, Louisiana

A very little water is a sea to an ant.

INDIAN PROVERB

Muir Inlet, Chilkat Range, Glacier Bay, Alaska

E arth is surprising. It has the self-contained look of a living creature. An organism in its own right, growing and changing, wrapping itself in a moist and luminous membrane. And this fluid, in itself, is rather odd.

Earth's aura, our humid air, is unlike any other atmosphere we know of. Almost everything about it violates the laws of chemistry. For a start it is composed largely of nitrogen and oxygen which, under most circumstances, is a highly combustible mixture. Nitrogen normally reacts with oxygen, and all or most of both gases should long since have ended up in the ocean in the form of some far more stable nitrate.

But our air stays stubbornly uncombined, with concentrations of oxygen and nitrogen at a steady and separate 21 and 78 percent respectively. Nor are these proportions arbitrary. If the abundance of oxygen was any greater, even by as little as 3 or 4 percent, everything would burst into flame. And if the level of nitrogen, which is largely responsible for air pressure, were to fall to seventy-five parts per hundred, temperatures would plummet. Nothing could prevent the onset of global, and possibly permanent, glaciation.

We know that the atmosphere began when the hot breath of our young planet bubbled up through cracks in the crust, throwing an odd collection of gases into an apparently random mechanical mixture, and that this blanket acted like the glass in a greenhouse, keeping earth reasonably warm.

But the way in which it has gone on doing so, despite the changes in our cosmic environment, suggests that air is something more than just a fortuitous emanation from some ancient rocks. It begins to look more and more like an artifact, like something made with, and sustained for, a purpose. And at the heart of this strange and active enterprise, lies water.

Water has an unusual capacity for storing heat. It soaks it up and moves it about, distributing it as evenly as possible. The ebb and flow of the great ocean mass ensures that even water from the bottom of the deepest trenches returns to the surface at regular intervals to pick up or discharge its thermal load. With the result that all the water in the world serves as an enormous flywheel, holding potential energy and releasing it at leisure later, bringing stability, even a sort of homeostasis, to the largest living creature in the solar system.

It helps to look at earth in this way. Ever since the Copernican revolution, which succeeded in breaking an ancient assurance that earth was the center of the universe, it has been regarded as almost heretical to suggest that our planet is special in any way. We are told that the galaxy contains several billions of planetary systems, and the chances are that these include millions of worlds like our own. Perhaps. But the many odd coincidences that surround us make it reasonable to feel at least a little geocentric.

We know now that the space between the stars is far from empty. It is studded with dust, some of it organic, a kind of sticky tar that contains all the necessary ingredients for life. And every day this planet collides with more than one hundred million bits out there, picking up enough extraterrestrial matter to have doubled our weight since the world began.

Web, Kintail Forest, Scotland

Condensation of water vapor takes place only when there is a suitable surface on which it can form. This can be the earth itself, as in the case of dew; but in free and perfectly clean air, rain is impossible. Nothing happens unless there are suitable nuclei, microscopic particles suspended in the air which attract molecules of water vapor. Fortunately, however, there are many. With at least one hundred tons of cosmic litter entering our atmosphere every day, it is not surprising that even the purest high-altitude air contains at least five thousand tiny particles of dust in every cubic inch. And with all this matter in solution raining down on earth, it would not be surprising if, as some scientists now suggest, our planet had been seeded very early in its history.

We do not live in a sealed spacecraft, isolated from the cosmos in a convenient bubble of air. We are exposed to the complex ecology of our galaxy and subject, like everything else in it, to ceaseless interchange. To constant bombardment by a host of raw materials. But, however one looks at it, it seems inevitable too that this matter has been shaped and molded here by circumstances that may well be unique. And not the least of these is the availability of lots of water, hovering unusually in the narrow range between its freezing and its boiling points. A warm and welcoming womb.

The first life on earth was certainly aquatic. It was, as far as we can tell, a simple protocell. Something like the large bacteria or solitary blue-green algae that still live in warm-water springs. Traces of it linger on as fossils in those granites of Africa and Australia that were formed 3,500 million years ago.

Our earliest ancestors clearly got together somewhere in a primordial sea. There is no telling how many times they tried, and failed, simply getting swallowed up and lost forever. But eventually there must have been enough of them to take root, to cope with a certain amount of attrition, and to grow and reproduce.

Reproduction is the big secret of life. An ability to manufacture others of one's kind. It implies the sort of control that simply doesn't exist anywhere else, even in elaborate organic chemistry. Amino acids are the essential precursors of life, but they are not in themselves, alive. They arise randomly and independently in nature, and can be produced in the laboratory by simulation of an early earth environment. But they cannot be persuaded to replicate themselves.

Such talents seem to depend on a kind of cohesion which becomes possible only when complex biochemicals like proteins enjoy a certain amount of privacy and protection. The kind that came with the development of the first cell wall—a thin, elastic membrane that separated some of life's machinery from the rigors of the world. A wall that grew and isolated parts of the ancient ocean, keeping them from the rest, creating areas of relative security.

It was in this way that our kind of life began. And the result is that each of us has become a mobile museum. We still carry that ancient ocean around inside us, trapped there like a living fossil forever.

Deer Creek Falls, Grand Canyon, Arizona

The fluid in our bodies is a perfect replica of that ocean in which we once grew to fruition. Parts of it have been permanently preserved, their contents protected from all the environmental changes that have taken place ever since. The concentration of chemicals in our blood and tissues are precisely the same as those that once prevailed in that embryonic sea.

In an atmosphere that, even at its most humid, never contains more than 3 percent of water, we are walking whirlpools, almost waterlogged. All living things are thus abundantly irrigated. Seventy-five percent of a chicken—more perhaps in some unscrupulous supermarkets—is liquid. Shrimps and prawns reach 80 percent. Tomatoes and lettuce are saturated with 95 percent or more. And it is a melancholy and dampening thought that even Raquel Welch is almost 70 percent water.

All cells are like this. They have to be. Metabolism depends on it.

Every cell has a fluid interior, a pool in which vital substances are dissolved. Paramount among these are hydrogen, oxygen, nitrogen, and carbon—the basic building blocks. But mixed with them are quantities of other chemicals such as magnesium, necessary for the construction of chlorophyll; iron, required for making red blood cells; phosphorus, the key element in all energetic equations; sulfur, which goes into fur and hoofs and horns; silica, holding up plants and providing translucent cases for some marine organisms; and calcium, which makes external armor for shellfish and gives mineral strength to stems and bones. The medley is compounded by essential traces of iodine, fluorine, chlorine, and bromine. And even by some silver, cobalt, vanadium, and gold.

Together, these chemicals produce the dazzling diversity of living things. And none of them could be used unless they were first dissolved in, and then transported by, water. With them in solution, all the magic happens.

85

Havasu Falls, Grand Canyon, Arizona

Taro, Kauai, Hawaii

The show begins on the waterfront, with plants, which tend to wallow in water. Something like six thousand cubic miles of it moves each year through plants, which cover earth's surface. This represents a volume of water almost equal to that which is carried to the sea by all the rivers of the world. Enough, if plants returned none of it, to drain the oceans in just two million years. But of course, the plant kingdom merely borrows the world's water and, in the process, taps the energy of sunlight to combine 25 billion tons of hydrogen from that water with 150 billion tons of carbon from the air, producing and releasing 400 billion tons of free oxygen. It is the cumulative effect of this great chemistry that not only makes air breathable, but creates all organic matter and feeds every living thing.

Wonderland Trail, Mount Rainier, Washington

The river of life runs through the trees. Literally. The cell walls in each root, stem, and leaf are the banks of this stream, which spouts from the top of every plant like a fountain. In one summer day, a single willow tree uses and loses over five thousand gallons of water. Forests create what amounts to an aerial ocean. An acre of corn produces more atmospheric vapor than a lake of the same size, sucking up and spitting out thirty-five hundred tons of water in a growing season, sufficient to flood its plot to a depth of over one foot. The figure for a crop of sugarcane is more like thirty feet, because it takes roughly two thousand pounds of water to make a pound of sugar.

Three-quarters of the weight of a living tree is water. Which, in a Douglas fir, can mean three hundred tons. But the amount of water retained is insignificant compared to the quantity used. More than one thousand pounds must pass through before the tree can build a pound of wood for itself. Annual plants, such as barley and oats, can be more economical, with ratios of five hundred to one. But, on average, all vegetation uses several hundred pounds of water in the production of a pound of its own dry weight. And when man interferes and cultivates, the process can be even more profligate. It takes twenty thousand gallons of water for us to produce every single bushel of wheat. Such prodigious thirsts turn every tree, each stalk of grass, into rivers that empty themselves endlessly into the air.

Transpiration is a fact, but the mechanism remains mysterious. We don't know exactly what it is that makes a plant a wick along which water moves from soil to sky.

Osmotic pressure, the difference in concentration of water molecules inside and outside a plant, creates a force that can lift a column of water ten feet up a tree. Capillarity, the attraction between water molecules, probably pushes it up another foot or two. But even taken together, these mechanisms fail to account for the fact that water somehow gets to the leaves of giant redwoods four hundred feet above the ground. The answer lies, perhaps, in the water itself.

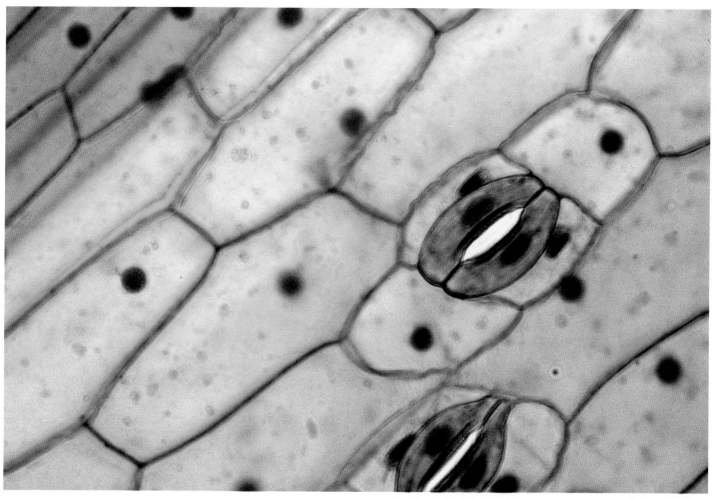

Stomata (160×)
Thin section courtesy of Dr. John Mecom, Richland College, Dallas, Texas. Equipment and technical assistance
courtesy of Dr. Judith Head, University of Texas Health Science Center, Dallas, Texas.

Each square inch of broad, green leaf contains up to three hundred thousand stomata—tiny vents flanked by sausage-shaped cells that flex when water makes them turgid, opening the pores and turning gas and vapor loose. Evaporation at these windows lowers the concentration of water in the leaf as a whole, pulling in extra molecules from the sap in a shoot. Which, in turn, makes demands on supplies lower down, until whole columns are put under tension.

90

Sycamore Tree, Bear Canyon Springs, Gila Wilderness, New Mexico

Water, fortunately, can take it. It is unique in its resistance to being pulled apart, having a tensile strength as great as many metals. As high, perhaps, as four thousand pounds per square inch. Enough to lift a column of sap trapped in slender vegetable tubes well over a thousand feet, twice the height of the tallest tree that ever lived.

All of which makes sense, but the problem doesn't end there. The trouble is that water continues to climb, sap goes on rising, even when a tree has shed its leaves and needs to feed its growing buds in spring.

The situation at the lower end of the plant pipeline is relatively simple. Except that roots go to extraordinary lengths to satisfy their thirst.

Most plants live within a few feet of a water table, but trees often reach down as much as eighty feet in search of a dependable supply. Others rely on profusion. Some kinds of desert cactus grow twenty miles of root and spread it, just beneath the surface, like a net designed to catch the first fruits of every rare and precious shower. Many come equipped with countless tiny root hairs which increase their absorbent surface. A single rye plant may have up to fifteen billion such retentive threads, with a total length of over three hundred miles.

The tip of all foraging roots is capped with a layer of hard dead cells that protect them as they probe the earth, pushing their way through cracks and crevices with an insistence that can be awesome. Roots in search of moisture are relentless, lifting paving, shifting houses, and splitting boulders that stand in their way. Until, eventually, they reach a water source and soak it up like blotters.

Outlined in this way, the process sounds destructive. But the truth is that, without these energetic tangles, there would probably be no fertile earth anywhere. It is the root systems that tie us down, stabilizing soil and staking out the slopes. Knitting grasslands and forests into continuous carpets, which prevent them, and everything living on them, from being washed and blown away.

92

Sequoia, California

Life is on a water course. The simpler forms remain immersed, while some more complex ones have managed to become relatively independent, colonizing the land, straying farther and farther from the shore. But even these are dedicated water carriers, with tissues that are essentially awash. Water flows through each of our cells, bringing warmth and nourishment and taking wastes away. We are all, more or less, waterlogged.

Insects are perhaps the most emancipated. Some beetles manage to survive with less than 50 percent of water in their bodies. But all the rest of us are at least two-thirds water. Frogs and toads, crabs and lobsters are, predictably, 80 percent afloat. While jellyfish are practically saturated. When these transparent umbrellas dehydrate on a sunny shore, nothing remains but a tacky residue—less than 3 percent of their total body weight.

Some fleshy plants and most fruits are just as liquid. Watermelons win with a colossal 97 percent, but some kinds of cabbage come in a close second with over 95. Apples and pineapples are in the 80s, along with potato tubers and earthworms. The tallest trees support their great weights with just 20 percent of their substance. While humans are, surprisingly, just as wet inside as any fish.

An average man carries 100 pounds of water in his 150-pound frame. That's ten gallons in all, two of which slosh in and out of the alimentary canal, lubricate our joints, and keep up the pressure in our eyeballs. Most of the rest flows through blood and muscle, but even our brains are 75 percent liquid. And it soaks into some other unexpected places. Bones, for instance, are far from dry, with 22 percent water, and there is another 2 percent in the enamel on our teeth.

All this moisture moves, working for our living. It percolates and diffuses through the body, which uses it again and again, irrigating itself with sixty thousand miles of arteries and veins, pushing our entire body volume through the kidneys every three minutes, cleansing something like four hundred gallons a day, flushing out wastes and excess salt in the three or four pints we lose in urine. Another pint disappears as moisture in the thirty thousand lungfuls of air we exhale each day. And a further pint or so seeps out through the surface of the skin as perspiration, or leaks down through the tear ducts after lubricating lids that sweep our eyeballs twenty-five times every minute.

These losses have to be made good. We can live several weeks without food—an Indian fakir once did so under observation for eighty-one days. But without water, we die in as little as three or four days. A drop of 2 percent in our body fluid immediately manifests itself as thirst or pain; a 5 percent loss induces hallucinations; and a loss of just 12 percent is lethal. Drinking returns roughly half of our needs. Another 15 percent we manufacture as a by-product of cell chemistry, and the rest we get with solid food, because even "dry" bread is 40 percent water.

There are a few species that seem to manage without water at all. Rodents, such as the kangaroo rat, conserve moisture by living underground, emerging only at night, and sweating and urinating very little. But they thrive in deserts largely because they have become water factories, making their own moisture by combining oxygen in the air with hydrogen from the carbohydrates in their food. They turn dry seeds to water and, once weaned, never need to drink again.

Anemone, Vancouver Island, British Columbia

Others beat the heat by storing water. Camels drink deeply when they can, soaking up as much as sixteen gallons at a time, adding a third to their body weight. This excess is not kept in bulk supply in stomach sacs or hump, but seeps into the tissues from which it can be easily withdrawn. On a long march, camels may go for more than two weeks without water and lose two hundred pounds, but they do so without dehydrating, diluting blood, or disturbing any of the essential body functions. Then they simply top up again. Humans use their body weight of water every four weeks; a camel makes the same turnover once in three months.

Cactus plants do even better. Their bodies swell like barrels after heavy rain, storing excess moisture in succulent tissue beneath a thick, waxy cuticle, and shrinking once again as they fall on harder times. A cactus can live for twenty-nine years on an amount of water equal to its own weight.

Barrel Cactus, La Désirade, Lesser Antilles

Navajo Mountain, Lake Powell, Utah

Around 16 percent of earth's land surface is true desert, without surface flow, permanent lakes, or any regular renewal of groundwater from local sources. The rest is more or less well watered, and therefore colonized.

Whether they come from the melt of snow or from a mountain spring, the headwaters of small springs are wonderfully cool. Their pools are open invitations to lie down and drink, and to peer into the tangle of delicately colored algae and mosses beneath the clear surface. Smooth, rocky shallows and riffles alternate with deeper areas where the water dams briefly against a glacial boulder and hardly seems to move at all. But most such streams are skittish in their youth, and the major problem facing life within them is to find some way of holding on against the flow.

Punchbowl Falls, Eagle Creek, Oregon

Upper Deer Creek Falls, Grand Canyon, Arizona

Plants tend to develop long and slippery streamers that float in the current like windblown hair. And animals, mainly the larvae of stone and caddis flies, grow sets of hooks and grapples to anchor themselves in the current. Where creeks tumble over sills and into even busier cascades, the eggs and larvae and pupae of other insects take advantage of the well-aerated water with a wonderful array of claws, cement glands, and suction cups. And at the feet of waterfalls, net-winged midges and assorted friends of the spray flourish among the moist stones and swales.

Downstream, things slow up a bit. The waters widen into pools overhung by sedge and grass, surrounded often by willow or alder. These shady basins are the haunt of salamanders and snails, and skitter with a profusion of tiny crustaceans, water fleas, and brightly colored water mites. They are, as a result, attractive too for frogs and snakes, and to brookside birds and mammals, the dippers and thrushes, the voles and water rats, that come to feed upon them.

Wedber Wood, North Yorkshire, England

North Channel Islands, Lake Huron, Ontario

The food web, the pyramid of who eats whom, goes on widening as inclines grow less steep and creeks mature, moving from V-shaped ravines out into more leisurely valleys. The crystal waters become progressively discolored, turning into tarns stained brown with humic acid and, later still, to streams muddy with suspended sediment.

In each case, the speed of flow determines whether the bottom will be pebble or sand; and the nature of this bed dictates the kind of plants that will grow there. As waters slow, silts settle, stems thicken, and leaves become progressively broader. Thickets of pond weed form and provide a greater variety of habitats. Crabs, flatworms, and mayfly larvae begin to abound, and this profusion feeds a panoply of fish that starts with gentle browsers and ends with the swirl and snatch of predators like trout and pike. And in their wake wait water shrews, a vigilant kingfisher or two, and the occasional otter.

Jo-Mary Lakes, Appalachian Trail, Maine

Wherever springs or streams flow into open country, their waters spread out into shallow bogs, swamps, fens, marshes, or mires. If the pause in their headlong flight to the sea is produced by a barrier, they may accumulate and deepen into lakes, but these never last very long. All lakes are doomed to die. Ooze has a tendency to build up on their bottoms, closing dark water eyes with an iris of green, growing from the edges in, until there is nothing left but moist and verdant land.

Such wetlands are the nurseries of natural history. Their shallow, rich, and relatively warm waters are brood chambers of enormous productivity. Ranging from bogs of acid water that grow up around patches of peat moss, through treeless marshes along river margins, to well-drained and more mature swamps in the shade of buttressed trees, all that these waterscapes have in common are their deoxygenated soils—and the fact that they are inundated for all or most of every year. But, as habitats, they are vital to our ecology and to our peace of mind.

103

Platte River Point, Michigan

Still waters have a soothing effect, a kind of poetic gravity, that seems to be good for our souls. And they tend to be floating gardens, teeming with life. More than half of the world's human population is now supported by rice, a domesticated swamp grass. Water meadows in Europe and the Americas feed many more. Everywhere, seasonal floods enrich and fertilize such land, encouraging the growth of sedge and papyrus, cattail, rush, and reed. Nurturing algal blooms that support mollusks and mosquitoes, breeding knotted masses of tubifex worms. And boiling, as a result, with carp and bass, with ducks and geese and soft-winged pelicans, crocodiles and alligators, mink and manatee, and even the occasional hippopotamus.

The story is the same from Florida's Everglades to the swamps of the Sudan, from Brazil's Pantanal to the Sepik in New Guinea. Wetlands more than earn their keep. They act as natural cushions, softening the shock of floods for those downstream. A million gallons is just four inches of water when it has been spread over ten acres of swamp. Water in such areas is in short-term storage, lingering there for a while before seeping through, cleansed of pollutants and impurities, filtered and refreshed on its way to the coast. Moving now, not as solitary streams, but more often in stately combination, as a river.

A river, almost by definition, is a body of moving water large enough to occupy one's mind. Something redolent of distant and legendary origins, filled with news of the sources from which it takes its strength. Rivers are metaphors for change, dreams of history. They move by, tangling the threads of time, braiding their waters into mixtures of the moment, open systems hinting at a single destiny—a predetermined and overwhelming need for the sea.

Colorado River, Marble Canyon, Arizona

On the same slope, large rivers flow faster than smaller ones, because there is less friction with their banks and beds. And, because even the air has a braking effect, the speed of any river's flow is greatest at a point somewhere between one-tenth and four-tenths of its depth below the surface. In addition, every bend and shift in direction, every rock and ledge below, produces whirls and upwellings which create random turbulence. The result is an environment where nothing is certain but change. A place for opportunists.

Plant life is confined to the edges, or to a few floating species that have solved their problems by developing spongy tissue filled with enough air to keep them at the surface. Animals have learned that, to stay in one place, they have to dig a hole, hug the bottom, or swim actively upstream. On sandy beds, mussels and crabs abound, siphoning food out of the soup passing by. Fish live at every level, often growing very large on the quantities of suspended raw material, which go on increasing all the way downstream. Until, finally, the whole rich soup slows down and spills over into an estuary.

Hecate Strait, Moresby Group, Queen Charlotte Islands, British Columbia

Shi Shi Beach, Olympic Peninsula, Washington

Neither land nor sea, estuaries are important to both. They are flood plains with funnel shapes, places where rivers begin to feel the rhythm of the tides. Vast mudflats, often protected from the open by sandspits and barrier beaches, where fresh and salt water mix reluctantly. Salt water is the heavier of the two, and rivers tend to flow out over wedges of the sea which protrude some way upstream. This tidal interface is complex, posing problems of adjustment for those that live along its gradient, but a constant supply of rich organic matter from far upstream guarantees that estuaries everywhere are among the most productive ecosystems in the world.

Planktonic algae at the base of the food chain support an enormous variety of mollusks, worms, crabs, shrimps, and fish. These dig down into the deltic oozes, throwing up serpentine castings in heaps upon the surface, lying low when the tide goes out and flats are besieged by a myriad of wading birds. Or they find shelter from sun, sandpiper, and plover in meadows of seagrass, clinging to the leafy branches and sorting the silt that builds up in these shallow pastures.

When estuaries are old enough, the flats become colonized by more mature communities of plants which decorate and stabilize a shore. Islands of vegetation form and grow, creating tangles at the edge of tidal creeks, trapping and holding yet more mud between their toes, feeding and housing another great host.

The result on cooler coasts is a salt marsh, a green and undulating sea of cordgrass, water thatch or marsh hay. A haven for clams and scallops, brackish-water fish, and dabbling duck. In the tropics, coasts are fringed instead with mangrove. Trees tolerant of salt, which prop themselves up on elevated roots in thickets rich in oysters, fiddler crabs, and mudskipping fish.

Mangroves, Everglades National Park, Florida

Estuaries are crossroads, meeting places on the margin of land and sea. Hotspots of evolution. Everyone there is on the way somewhere else. Eels pass through, sleek and fat and silver, in compulsive flight back to the sea to spawn. But most of us seem, like salmon, to be going the other way.

Humans can, on the whole, be said to be drying out. We begin our individual lives immersed in liquid in the womb. A three-day-old fetus is still 97 percent water, as wet as any jellyfish, but by eight months old this falls to 81 percent. As adults, we stabilize at around 65 or 70 percent; although women, with more fatty tissue, which is largely water-free, may fall as low as 50. But as a species, in both sexes and in almost every aspect of our lives, we betray our essentially aquatic origins.

We are, for a start, the only naked apes. Our very short, fine body hair suggests that something happened in human history that didn't affect the ancestors of either gorillas or chimpanzees. It could have been a need to keep cool during the rigors of a hunt out on the savannah, but running away from predators generates just as much heat as running after prey. And there are, anyway, no naked leopards or cheetahs. It could have been a way of dealing with unruly body parasites, but even notably lousy animals like wolves and badgers cling resolutely to their fur.

The only reasonable explanation is the one that links us with other hairless mammals, like dolphins and hippos, who are more or less permanently wet. It makes sense to assume that we too once spent a lot of our time in water, keeping only the hair on our heads—partly as protection against the sun, but also to give our water babies something convenient to cling to on an otherwise slippery body. It seems significant that women, who are most involved in such nurturing, should be less prone to baldness and have scalps that grow particularly thick and luxurious anchors just when they happen to be pregnant.

We also resemble marine mammals without hair in that we insulate our bodies instead with a layer of subcutaneous fat. No other land animal does that. They may store excess energy in humps or pot bellies, but never grow fat thighs or cheeks or fingers. This sort of general distribution of body fat makes sense only for an animal that swims a lot and needs to be both streamlined and buoyant.

We are also extraordinarily leaky. All mammals lubricate their eyes with small amounts of secretion, but only seals and humans weep salty tears. Some mammals keep areas of exposed skin on their paws, feet, or noses supple with a secretion from special glands, but only humans sweat profusely. With two thousand glands per square inch of skin, we lose a pint or more of liquid every day and can, when walking unclad and unwisely in the sun, shed gallons and suffer from significant salt loss. None of which makes sense unless one assumes that we once had a salt problem and needed to get rid of an excess acquired as a result of living in the sea.

But perhaps the best evidence of water in our history is the fact that human babies swim, naturally and easily, long before they ever learn to sit up or crawl.

In their first year of life, babies are perfectly happy with their heads submerged. They behave calmly, gazing around with wide open eyes, showing no sign of fear, paddling easily up to the surface whenever they need to breathe. They never ever try to do so with their heads underwater. It seems to be only later that we lose these instincts and become more prone to drowning. Which seems unnecessary, because as a species we are unique among land animals in that we have a "dive reflex," a marked reduction in heart rate and oxygen consumption, which takes over automatically as soon as water touches our faces. We all have rudimentary webs between our fingers and thumbs, and as many as 7 percent of human beings in all cultures are still born with distinctively webbed feet.

And we speak. A fact that sets us apart from the rest of the animal kingdom and is very difficult to explain.

Most other monkeys communicate by sight and smell. A few do use vocal signals, but we alone have acquired conscious and voluntary control over the air channels that power the larynx in our throats. We can seal parts of the air passage off from others and produce a variety of nasal sounds and some clicks and stops that only dolphins can duplicate. Perhaps because they, like we, have had to learn the same kind of rigorous breath control during diving.

The list grows, and the evidence becomes difficult to ignore. We have so many special characteristics that become reasonable and normal only when compared with those of aquatic mammals. Then we make sense. We must have enjoyed our own aquatic interlude. Why not? It has happened before.

A long time before the first mammals came into being, an air-breathing, land-living dinosaur went back into the sea and stayed there long enough to grow flippers. These "fish lizards" are common in the fossil record. It is even possible that some still survive. In 1981, an expedition from the University of Chicago reported seeing something very like such a giant aquatic reptile in the Likouala region of the Republic of the Congo.

Seventy million years ago, a group of warm-blooded early hoofed animals, grazing on the banks of tropical rivers, took to the water—much as hippopotamuses still do. They evolved to fill an ecological niche left open by the sudden disappearance of most of the ruling reptiles, and it was the descendants of these opportunists that became whales and dolphins.

Twenty million years later, it was the turn of the elephant family. That transition gave rise to the sea cows, the ones we now know as manatees and dugongs. And around thirty million years ago, it was relatives of the bears and dogs that submerged themselves to become seals, otters, and beavers.

If reptiles, ungulates, and carnivores—not to mention birds, insectivores, marsupials, and rodents—can all take to the water, why not a primate? And if one did, it seems only reasonable to assume that it would have adapted in much the same way. Giving rise to the noisy, sweaty, weepy, naked apes that we call people.

The search for evidence goes on. There is nothing yet to show where or what we were just before small bipedal humanoids took to living on the floor of the Great Rift Valley, leaving their evocative footprints in soft lakeside muds. But it seems likely that many of our most distinctive traits derive from a time spent in or near the water, probably on the shores of an African estuary. A place where we would have had access to both the balm of fresh water and to the bounty of the sea.

We know from the evidence of old marine terraces that the ocean level changed dramatically about ten million years ago. The sea came flooding in and inundated East Africa's coastal plains, breaking the shore up into huge bays of shallow water that turned isolated hills into offshore islands. Populations marooned in such places would soon have run out of their usual forest foods and been forced to take to the water, changing their diet and their way of life, relying more and more on what they could find along the new shorelines.

The floods ended only with the arrival, about five million years ago, of hotter, drier times. The sea retreated and left the aquatic apes, now walking upright as a result of spending so much time hanging vertically in the water, free to adapt yet again. Which they seem to have done very successfully, leaping ahead of their landbound relatives, who went straight from the forest to the savannah without benefit of an immersion in between.

It could be deep memories of that baptism, of a time of trial and transition, that lie behind all our myths and legends of a great deluge.

We are born in water and become waterborne.

116

Composite: Silhouette, Queen Charlotte Islands, British Columbia/Sunset, Hawksbill Beach, Antigua, Lesser Antilles/Sunset, Kaibab Plateau, Arizona

Part Three

WATER AND SCIENCE

Shipwreck, Isle of Eigg, Scotland

Water can both float and sink a ship.
    Chinese Proverb

Cleft Waterfall, Isle of Eigg, Scotland

Water is the most common liquid in the world. In fact, it is the *only* liquid common to our planet. And yet it was not really recognized until the eighteenth century.

Before that, water was merely known and largely taken for granted. Thales of Miletus, the earliest of Greek philosophers, believed that it was the original substance of the universe, from which all else derived. The earth, he suggested, was a disk floating on water inside a hemisphere of stars which, in turn, drifted on an endless ocean. He was clearly aware of water's three natural states, describing the properties and uses of each in detail. "Water is best," he said with satisfaction.

Those who followed him were content, on the whole, to leave it at that. Empedocles in the fifth century B.C. added fire, earth, and air to water as basic elements. And Aristotle, a century later, made the necessary biological connection with his observation that the seeds of everything had a "moist nature." Water, he concluded, was definitely the first principle of life.

119

And there it rested for two thousand years. Until an accident in 1783.

Benjamin Franklin had flown his kite and everyone was talking about electricity. A few were even doing something about it. In England, Henry Cavendish was passing electric current through a variety of substances to see what happened to the voltage. It varied at the electrodes, usually without affecting the conductor in between. But when he filled a sealed glass tube with water and sent his current through this, the result was completely unexpected. The water vanished.

Cavendish was astounded. Convinced that the tube must have a leak, he repeated the experiment again and again, until he was certain that it was airtight. There was no mistake. The water had been turned, instantly, into an invisible gas. And when he analyzed the contents of the tube, Cavendish found that it contained a mixture of two gases, one of which was his old friend "inflammable air." The other was a heavier gas, one discovered a few years earlier by his colleague Joseph Priestley who, finding that it supported combustion and kept a mouse alive, called it "vital air."

All that remained was for Cavendish to put the constituents back together again. Which he did by mixing a measured volume of inflammable air with different volumes of its vital counterpart, and setting fire to the two. Most of the mixtures burned well enough, but when the proportions were precisely two to one, there was an explosion and the walls of his container were covered with liquid droplets. These he quickly identified as water.

Black Sand Geyser Basin, Yellowstone, Wyoming

Water, announced Cavendish, was not water. Not just an odorless, tasteless, and colorless substance that lay beyond the reach of chemical analysis. Not an element in its own right that flowed about the world, passing through its phases, evaporating and condensing and being born again and again. But a compound of two independent elements, one combustible and the other a supporter of combustion, which together united to become the paramount quencher of flames and thirst.

A few years later, the great Frenchman Antoine Lavoisier tied the parcel neatly together by renaming the constituents *hydrogen*—"the water producer"—and *oxygen*. And when this distinguished scientist fell victim to the Revolution and was ultimately guillotined, his tombstone came to carry a simple and telling epitaph, a fitting tribute to the father of new chemistry— just two *H*'s and one *O*.

121

H_2O was a revelation. The splitting of the molecule of water into its parts led to a new philosophy, a breakthrough in scientific thought. John Dalton was just eighteen years old when Cavendish did his vanishing trick, but by 1808 he was in a position to publish a treatise on the atomic nature of matter. A work in which the understanding of intuitive ancient Greeks such as Democritus was finally put to the test; and which has, in our day, led directly to the harnessing of atomic energy and the exploration of space.

We are cavalier now about the matter. Every high school student knows that water is a chemical compound of two simple and abundant elements. And yet scientific journals continue to carry articles arguing the merits of rival theories on the structure of water. We still do not know exactly how it works.

Nobody has ever seen a water molecule. All we have are theoretical diagrams and equations. The formula H_2O is disarmingly simple, but the reality is very complex. From X-ray studies, we know that the atoms in water are intricately laced. Interconnections between them are so profuse that some workers go so far as to describe an entire river, all the way from its headwaters to the sea, as a single molecule tied together by countless billions of tiny bonds.

Water is almost indestructible. As Cavendish found out, electrolysis can separate its atoms, but once two hydrogen atoms and one oxygen atom get together, they need to be heated up to twenty-nine hundred degrees Celsius to prize them apart again. With the result that water created three billion years ago is still in existence, moving restlessly from state to state, flowing intact down the corridors of time.

123

Colorado River Riffle, Grand Canyon, Arizona

Loch Eil, Carn Mor Dearg, Ben Nevis, Scotland

The secret of water's resilience lies in its hydrogen atoms and their bonds. Hydrogen is the smallest atom of all. It has only one negatively charged electron to share with any other atom with which it combines, but because of its size it can get very near to its neighbors. And does so, putting its positively charged nucleus so close to oxygen's electrons that the magnetic attraction between them is unusually strong. It is also very strange.

Instead of attaching themselves randomly to each oxygen atom, the two atoms of hydrogen in a water molecule take up a very precise and idiosyncratic alignment to each other. Most molecules adopt a regular geometry, building up at angles of 45, 60, or 90 degrees that make it possible for them to be equally spaced and neatly arranged. Not water. The two hydrogen atoms *always* come to rest at an angle of exactly 104.5 degrees from each other, making all diagrams of their attachment to the larger oxygen atom look like ears on the round head of a panda.

There is nothing to account for this peculiarity, no explanation that as yet makes sense. But it is crucial to all life on earth. It is the angle of life, the secret that lies behind everything, from the magic of natural spirals in a molecule of DNA to the pattern of pine cones, the architecture of a snail shell, and the shape at the center of a daisy.

The answer is 104.5. All we have to do now is to pose all the proper questions.

Water is lopsided. And, as a result, highly eccentric, breaking all the rules.

The laws of physics require that matter becomes more dense as its temperature falls and it shifts from gas to liquid and finally to a solid state. Most materials do so. But not water, which behaves in the expected manner only until its temperature reaches 4 degrees Celsius. Then something weird happens. Instead of shrinking further, water suddenly starts to expand, until at zero—the traditional freezing point—it has grown in volume by as much as 11 percent. Which is why boulders crack, sidewalks buckle, and pipes and radiators burst on cold winter nights. And why there is still life left anywhere on earth at all.

As they cool, all molecules slow up and begin to crowd together. Because of the angle of life, those of water drift naturally, in groups of five, into regular polygons which become braced by their bonds before they reach their minimum size. With the result that solid water, or ice, is an open, porous structure with fewer molecules in the same space. It is less dense and therefore floats on liquid water. Which is just as well. If it were not so, ice would sink, and it would not be long before every pond and pool, every arm of the ocean, was solid, freezing from the bottom up.

Once this happened, all earth's water would be locked away and there could be no wells or springs, no streams or brooks, no humidity and no rain. Nothing but an ice age that went on forever.

It is only water's physical oddity that prevents such a disaster.

Not least of water's peculiarities is the fact that, as a liquid, it is actually more like a solid.

Riggs Glacier, Glacier Bay National Park, Alaska

The bonds in it are rigid and prescribed. The angle of 104.5 degrees between hydrogen atoms is mirrored in the regular arrangement between water molecules, which come to lie in groups of five, as they do in crystals of ice. In fact, liquid water seems to consist of numbers of such tiny crystals, each one existing only for an instant, forming and dissolving many millions of times a second. It is as though the liquid remembers what it was like to be ice, and flows about muttering under its breath, repeating the essential formula to itself again and again, ready to change back at a moment's notice.

As a liquid, water is rather chaotic, its molecules pressing in together in constantly shifting confusion. But as a solid, it calms down somewhat as the bonds become more rigid bridges, opening up spaces between them and making the substance, although solid, altogether less dense.

Which is why ice floats and why it melts, turning back to a liquid under pressure, lubricating the runners of ice skates while the actual temperature is still too low to bring about a natural change of state.

Ice is a very busy molecule, with many liquid properties. A reminder that lines between the solid, liquid, and gaseous states of water are imprecisely drawn.

Iceberg, Muir Remnant, Glacier Bay, Alaska

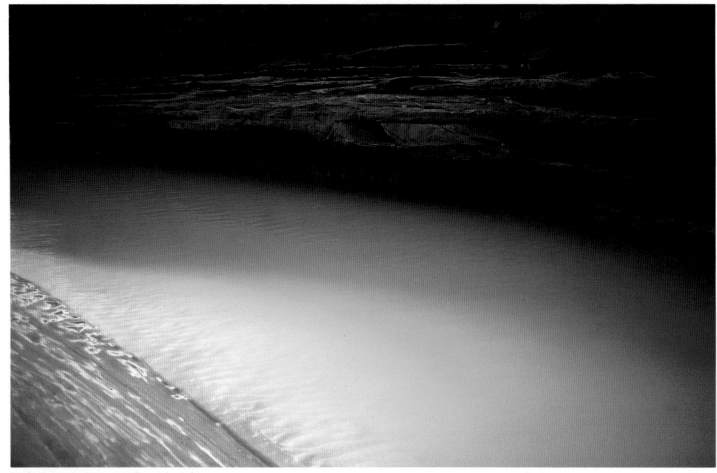

Little Colorado River (confluence), Arizona

Water, in any of its forms, also has scant respect for the laws of chemistry.

Most materials act either as acids or bases, settling on either side of a natural reactive divide. Not water. It is one of the few substances that can behave both as an acid and as a base, so that under certain conditions it is capable of reacting chemically with itself. Or with anything else.

Molecules of water are off balance and hard to satisfy. They reach out to interfere with every other molecule they meet, pushing its atoms apart, surrounding them, and putting them into solution. Water is the ultimate solvent, wetting everything, setting other elements free from the rocks, making them available for life. Nothing is safe. There isn't a container strong enough to hold it. Seconds after distilled water is caught in a beaker, it is contaminated by molecules of glass.

Water is not only active, but inert. Every lake and stream in the world is a natural solution. The oceans abound in dissolved matter, becoming quite concentrated soups of thousands of substances, including enough gold to make every person in the world a millionaire. But the water that acts as such a universal solvent is not itself changed in any way. It goes on working again and again, round and round forever.

Such hyperactivity is essential. It is because water keeps so astonishingly busy that minerals can pass from soil into the roots of plants, and flow from there up into their stems and flowers. Water's restlessness is responsible for the digestion of food and the movement of nourishment into our bloodstreams. And it carries life-giving gases across the moist membranes of leaves and in and out of our lungs. Without such traffic, life would long since have ground to an arid halt.

Stone Creek, Grand Canyon National Park, Arizona

Sandwood Stream, Sutherland, Scotland

Water is also coherent. It sticks to itself. Raindrops on a window run irresistibly into each other, building up a liquid lattice. Molecules at the edge of any quantity of water have a strong mutual attraction, clinging together to form a highly flexible coat of liquid chain mail. And this elasticity allows a film of water to bulge like a balloon, pulling away from a leaf tip or a bathroom tap, stretching under its own weight, gradually elongating, until it breaks loose and snaps around a free-falling drop. The skin, however, never tears. Under gravity, it simply closes over the margins, turning the drop into a perfect sphere.

This is surface tension, and water has more of it than any other liquid except mercury.

It takes an astonishing amount of force to break the tension. A film of water, just one molecule thick, readily supports the weight of a host of insects which stride and skate and row across its surface. The sheet is taut enough to keep a needle or a flat metal plate afloat, but even when such objects sink, each one is instantly wrapped in a tightly fitting skin. So that every human diver and every sunken ship is modeled and outlined in water, displacing a volume precisely equal to its own body weight.

Water grabs at everything. It grasps for the edges of particles in porous soil, reaching out with wet and sticky fingers, pulling itself along hand over hand. It clings to the molecules of other substances and, once attached, hauls itself up like a boat warping upstream, moving against the tide, holding tight even to the smooth walls of veins and arteries and the mirror surfaces of glass tubes.

This is capillarity, a special talent that makes it possible for water to creep uphill. It does so even at the edges of large water surfaces, but is at its most impressive in fine tubes, where a high percentage of molecules are in touch with the sides. Then it climbs the walls, wetting the wicks of the world, moving up the tubes in tall trees, creeping through to even the most remote cells in a tissue, stopping only when gravity calls a halt.

Capillary action makes water not only physically and chemically unique, but biologically indispensable. Without it, circulation would cease and life become impossible.

Windshield in the Rain, Austin, Texas

There is, in addition, something very odd about the way water behaves in the presence of heat.

Judged only by its molecular weight, water should freeze at minus 100 degrees Celsius and boil at minus 80. Fortunately for us, it doesn't, or blood would boil in our bodies and there would be nothing on earth but superheated steam. As it is, water moves between zero and plus 100 degrees, passing through all three of its phases within the narrow range of temperatures naturally found on earth. You can see water as solid, liquid, and gas simultaneously around a single pond in winter.

In most substances, the amount of heat needed to increase their temperature by one degree is the same with each degree involved. But not so with water. Between 35 and 40 degrees Celsius, water is unusually relaxed and most easily warmed. And this narrow range just happens to coincide, if you believe in such accidents, with the usual body temperature of most active animals. This is not only convenient but may be vital. It could even be the trigger that makes all living things so wonderfully responsive to their environment.

It has been known for some time that chemical reactions can be erratic. Sometimes they work, sometimes they don't. The vagaries are not usually sufficient to cause concern, but a few industries are sensitive enough to need to avoid such aberrations. And research among these has revealed the existence of factors well beyond normal laboratory control. Reactions involving some solutions change as the water in them adapts itself to very delicate and distant influences, responding to shifts in earth's magnetic field or to the frequency of spots on the sun.

The mechanics of such responses are still poorly understood, but it is becoming clear that water is much more than a convenient solvent or an aid to digestion. Its flexibility and sensitivity, which are highest around normal body temperature, make it an ideal go-between. And its presence in abundance in everybody makes it a useful and convenient trigger substance. A point of contact between life and the cosmos. Something that amounts almost to a separate sense organ.

Water Strider, Garnet Canyon, Arizona

Plug Vortex, Dallas, Texas

Water is certainly impressionable. A breeze blowing over it creases the surface into responsive ripples. A stone thrown into it creates a pattern which passes rhythmically on to the entire fabric. The great oscillations of the tides are echoes that resound to an interplay of earth and cosmos. And, on a smaller level, it is the elastic surface of water in a sink or tub that takes on peaceful curves and runs away in a beautiful spiral vortex. This turns alternately left or right, depending on the last force to touch it.

But perfectly still water naturally reflects the motion of the earth, turning clockwise in the northern hemisphere and counterclockwise in the south.

All water boundaries act as receptors, picking up signals as living membranes do. Like many membranes, their receptivity improves when they themselves are in motion, capable of making waves of their own that set up interference patterns. A stream bubbling over stones forms countless inner surfaces and tiny vortices, each one tuned to a different wavelength. And water so sensitized may be capable of passing received impressions on to other living things.

Forest at Windy Bay, Lyell Island, Queen Charlotte Islands, British Columbia

There is some evidence to suggest that water shaken up in a sealed container during an environmental crisis, such as a solar eclipse, is different. When fed to wheat seedlings, it provides less nourishment and results in less growth than water from similar containers that were shaken either before or after the event.

It may be necessary to begin to think of water as an organism in its own right, as a creature that metabolizes, moving more quickly when it is warm and less dense, putting out new feelers, opening up extra sense organs as it flows from a cool forest glade out into the sunlit expanse of a summer meadow.

Small differences in temperature can have dramatic effects on water.

On the banks of a deep pool in a mountain stream, a young Austrian forester once had an almost mystical experience. The night was clear and the moon was full, and looking down through the crystal waters, Viktor Schauberger was astonished to see large, egg-shaped stones begin to move on circular paths and float right up to the surface.

He was aware that motion in water has the effect of "concentrating" it, giving certain areas a slightly greater density. An egg, for instance, whose specific gravity is only marginally higher than water, will rise to the surface in a glass if the liquid is stirred in a certain way. And though it takes more force to float a rock, Schauberger realized that he wasn't imagining things. In a pool of the right shape, on a cold night, with strongly flowing water already near its point of maximum density at four degrees, stones could indeed be induced to dance.

As a forester, Schauberger was involved in logging and well aware of the difficulty of operating chutes in areas where there was too little water or an insufficient slope. Starting in 1920, he began to put his nocturnal insight to work, building revolutionary new chutes in which he gave a little water a lot of power by helping it to assume the serpentine and swirling flow he had seen in that mountain pool.

Strathcona Provincial Park, Vancouver Island, British Columbia

Schauberger made his chutes of wood, gave them egg-shaped cross sections, and nailed baffles and guides into curves in the flume to impart a special spin to the flow. He used the coldest water he could find, introducing new and cooler liquid at carefully spaced mixing points all along the line. And he ignored conventional wisdom, which insisted that flumes should travel by the shortest and quickest route downhill, letting his follow easy and natural meanders all the way to their destination.

The results were sensational. Everywhere he worked, Schauberger moved logs when no one else could manage it. Others copied his techniques but could never get them to work properly until he himself came in and made a few delicate and incomprehensible adjustments, altering the water temperature, perhaps, by just one-tenth of a degree.

Viktor Schauberger died in 1958 and the last of his amazing chutes was demolished shortly afterward. Much of the magic died with him, but his ideas have begun to help us to look at water in a new and more enlightened way.

Metz's Garden, Coshocton, Ohio

Anyone who has tasted natural spring water knows that it is different from city water, which is used over and over again, passing from mouth to laboratory and back to mouth again, without ever being allowed to touch the earth. We need to practice such economies these days, but in several thirsty countries, there are now experts in hydrodynamics who are trying to solve the problem by designing flowforms that copy the earth, producing rhythmic and spiral motions in moving water. And these pulsations do seem to vitalize and energize the liquid in some way, changing its experience, making it taste different and produce better crops.

The nature of the change is difficult to measure and remains mysterious. But it is no longer quite so outrageous to speak of "living water," or to suggest that water can grow and mature or, if treated badly, even die.

The contact with earth remains an important one. In the mountains of Bavaria, some high-forest farmers managed to grow consistently better crops of oats and potatoes than their neighbors. And all these successful cultivators practice an ancient rite known as *Tonsingen*. Around sunset each day of the growing season, they can be found leaning over a bucket of water, stirring a little clay into it with a wooden spoon—and singing. As they stir, they let their voices rise and fall, impressing the pattern of the chant on the water surface in a liquid lullaby, before putting the buckets away in the dark. At dawn the next day, this water is sprinkled over the fields in a ritual baptism.

Superstitious nonsense? Maybe. It is certainly hard to justify such practices in physical or chemical terms. Science sees no difference in the water. But the fact remains that those who serenade theirs enjoy a 30 percent greater yield than neighbors using ordinary water on the same seed and soil.

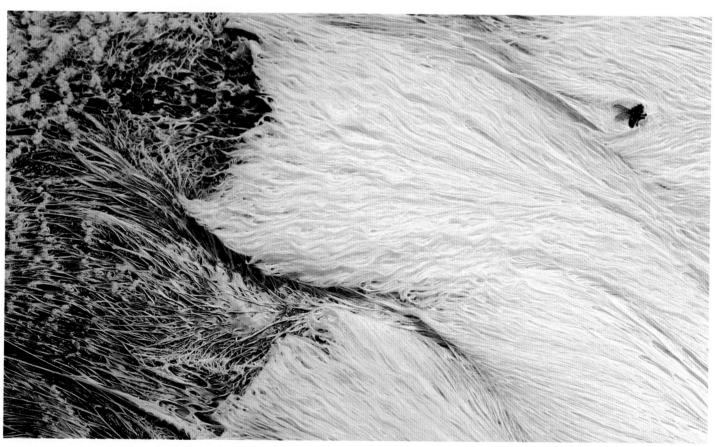

Thermal Bacteria Strands (and indigenous fly), Yellowstone, Wyoming

We are left with yet another mystery, and with a growing awareness that water is not just water. It is a vital substance, earth's blood, something of rich and infinite variety.

There is no such thing as pure water. All of it consists of two *H*'s and one *O*, but the elements themselves can vary.

Hydrogen usually has an atomic weight of one, but it also occurs naturally in two other forms, or isotopes, which are slightly heavier, with weights of two and three. And oxygen, whose normal atomic weight is sixteen, can be found as isotopes with weights of seventeen or eighteen. Since each of the three kinds of hydrogen joins with each of the three oxygens in the ratio of two to one, there are eighteen possible combinations with molecular weights that range from eighteen to twenty-four. The chemical formula remains the same, but the properties differ wildly, making water a very complex compound indeed.

The best known of these variations is the one that has two hydrogen atoms with twice the normal weight. This is *heavy water*. It has a freezing point of 3.8 degrees Celsius and a boiling point of 101.4, and is quite unlike ordinary water in a number of other ways. Seeds watered with it never germinate. And animals that drink it die of thirst. It is physiologically inert and fortunately forms only a minute fraction, around one in seven thousand parts, of water in the wild; but it has become increasingly important as a moderator in nuclear stations, where it slows down chain reactions.

Other variants occur naturally as a result of electrical changes, but a few have only been produced as laboratory curiosities. In 1969, by putting a fine column of water under unusual pressure, scientists manufactured an aberration they called *polywater*. This freak was very dense and refused to freeze until it was 40 degrees below zero. The boiling point was an amazing 415 degrees Celsius. There was concern at first lest this monster get loose, feed on natural water and go on doing so until all earth became totally uninhabitable. But it seems now that something rather like it might occur anyway in protoplasm, where it increases viscosity in useful ways.

141

Deer Creek, Grand Canyon National Park, Arizona

It is a sobering thought that the water we drink with such impunity should be the most corrosive liquid known.

The problem is its own thirst. Water is always grasping at other substances, gathering these around it, never content to be just H_2O. Half the known elements in the world are dissolved in our lakes and seas. And it is these additions that add to water's own amazing range and flexibility.

Water on its own doesn't conduct electricity at all. It actually makes an excellent insulator. But in contact with air or soil, it picks up electrolytes such as carbon dioxide so rapidly that it soon becomes suicidal to handle any kind of power while standing on a surface that is merely moist. Electricians even have problems with humid air.

The addition of some chemicals to water can realign its molecules, changing the way in which they behave. One new technique involves a tiny trace of lubricant, scarcely enough to be measured, which makes water more than usually mobile, less susceptible to friction. This *slippery water* travels faster, allowing the same volume to be moved through smaller apertures in lighter tubes and nozzles. It is proving a boon to hard-pressed fire fighters, battling with the older, heavy hoses on stairs of high-rise buildings in our cities.

Such substances are tied to water's hydrogen bonds, but molecular union isn't necessary. Water's tastes are so catholic and all-embracing that it will go along even with substances to which it is not attracted at all. And this can cause problems.

In contact with the larger molecules of most proteins, water's bonds are weakened. The tension that holds its molecules together is relaxed, and they move farther apart. With the result that liquid water becomes less dense; in other words, it turns to solid and freezes. And ice crystals form in such places as the leaves of plants, causing frost damage when the air temperature is still well above freezing.

In another instance, water mixed with methane in pipelines carrying natural gas has its freezing point raised so high that pipes have been known to become clogged with "snow" even on summer days with the temperature at 20 degrees Celsius.

143

West Shore, Antigua, Lesser Antilles

Compared with all other substances, water has an immense capacity for absorbing and storing heat. It takes a lot of energy to raise water's temperature in the first place. While an empty pot above a fire soon glows red-hot, one filled with water may become only a few degrees warmer during the same length of time. But it is just as reluctant to give up that hard-won heat. With the result that any body of water behaves like a hot-blooded being, keeping those around it warmer than they would otherwise be.

Ocean currents from the tropics cosset colder shores. Big ones like the Gulf Stream, which moves twenty-five times more water than all the rivers of the world combined, change entire climates, making Norwegian coasts ten degrees warmer than they should be at that latitude. But even a small volume of warm water can have a dramatic effect. A tub of it in a greenhouse on a cold winter night will be partly frozen by morning, but the heat it gives off in the process will keep the air inside that house warmer than the air outside.

This is latent heat, and water has more of it than any other substance on earth. It is an energy sponge. As it moves from solid to liquid at its melting point, there is a pause, as for a while the two phases coexist. As long as they do, heat is absorbed without a change in temperature. Which is why ice is so useful for refrigeration. As it melts, it draws heat from its surroundings.

And the same thing happens when water vaporizes. As it moves from liquid state to gas, there is another pause. Until all the liquid is gone, heat is absorbed without water molecules becoming agitated enough to raise its temperature. Which is why hot, dry air passing over a wet surface gives up its heat so readily, making for efficient air-conditioning. And why so much of earth is habitable. With 120,000 cubic miles of water evaporating all over the world each year, and enough of it falling again to cover Texas to a depth of 2,800 feet, we are all water-cooled.

Changes in the opposite direction, from gas to liquid, or from liquid to solid, involve an equivalent release of energy. There is enough in just one gallon of water to keep a standard sixty-watt bulb burning for over 375 hours. Which is why water is the prime source of energy in most power stations, and why it is still used for fuel cells in the generators aboard spacecrafts. And why thunderheads in summer boil over into powerful convection currents, exploding with more energy than an atomic bomb, producing awesome displays as water vapor condenses into visible raindrops.

145

Old Faithful Geyser, Yellowstone, Wyoming

Water molecules are a little like insects on a day in early spring. They move faster and become more energetic as they pick up heat. And go on accelerating until some are traveling fast enough to take off. These reach escape velocity and shoot right through the film of surface tension into orbit.

Some molecules of water manage to do this when the temperature is relatively low. Evaporation takes place over a pond even in winter. But as water temperature increases, more and more molecules break loose, until there are so many on the way up and out that the surface is not large enough to accommodate them all. Then some of them vaporize down below, and water boils.

At a normal atmospheric pressure of around thirty inches of mercury, water boils at 100 degrees Celsius. As pressure falls, the molecules become more easily excited. They have the space to move, and boiling takes place at lower temperatures. At an altitude of ten thousand feet, water boils at 90 degrees, and it becomes difficult to cook an egg or make a decent cup of tea. On top of Mount Everest, it is impossible. Water boils there at just 72 degrees Celsius.

147

Tundra (Autumn), Denali National Park, Alaska

Punchbowl Springs, Yellowstone, Wyoming

Under certain circumstances, water can be heated above 100 degrees Celsius without turning to steam. If it is kept absolutely still, which is difficult to do, the molecules experience a kind of inertia and don't escape until the temperature rises to 105 or 106 degrees. In one carefully staged experiment, water was actually heated to 178 degrees without boiling, but then it made up for lost time. It broke free from the artificial restraints and boiled with explosive violence, vaporizing almost instantaneously.

When pressure is increased, as it is inside the boiler of a steam engine, the boiling point of water rises. But its volume remains much the same.

Liquid water is almost incompressible. If atmospheric pressure is doubled, water volume decreases by only 0.005 percent. In a teacup, this is negligible. But if it didn't take place at all, the level of the sea would be 120 feet higher than it is today and another ten million square miles of land would be submerged.

The total quantity of water on earth is much the same now as it was more than three billion years ago, when the 326 million cubic miles of it were first formed. Ever since then, the pool has gone round and round, cooling, warming, building up, and breaking down. It is very durable, but remains difficult to define, because it has never been isolated in a completely pure state.

Chemically, water is hydrogen protoxide. But it turns out on more sophisticated analysis to be a mixture of as many as thirty-three possible compounds. And all its physical constants are abnormal.

Water has no nutritive value. And yet it is the major constituent of all living things.

Water is used to fight fires. Yet we spray coal in a furnace with water in order to make it burn better.

Some substances that contain water cannot be persuaded to part with it below a temperature of 2,900 degrees. While others that do not contain water will liberate it when even gently heated.

The list is endless. The anomalies go on and on. Only one thing is certain. As far as science is concerned, water may be common, but it is far from commonplace.

151

Whiten Peninsula, Sutherland, Scotland

Stones at Callanish, Scotland

Part Four

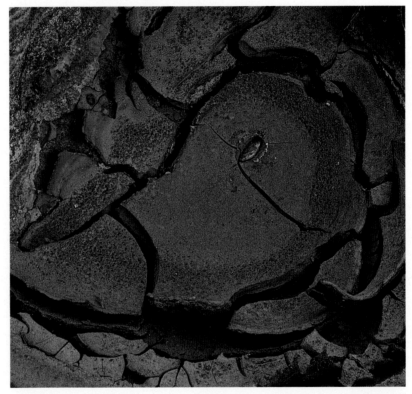

WATER AND HISTORY

Mud Cracks, Carbon Creek, Grand Canyon, Arizona

We never miss the water till the well runs dry.

ENGLISH PROVERB

154

Nebo Pass and the Grenadiers, Colorado

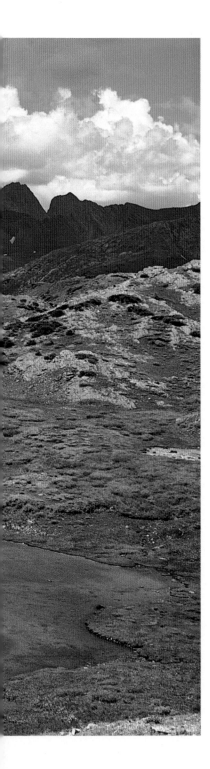

Drinking places are dangerous. They always have been. All animals approach them with caution, and a very large proportion die there nonetheless, ambushed by a lurking predator. The rule is, drink and run, and live to drink again. Which is fine as far as it goes, but it is very limiting.

We celebrate the birth of speech, the conquest of fire, and the invention of the wheel. These were indeed high points in our history. But a moment just as seminal came with the discovery that water could be stored and carried and used later, somewhere else. In a place of greater safety.

The first water containers were probably natural ones, gourds or shells emptied of their contents, filled perhaps with sponges of moss and plugged by a convenient stick or pebble. It sounds simple, but it was a turning point in our evolution. A true watershed. A huge stride away from the ties of riverbanks and beaches into new and more challenging environments.

Equipped with their own private pools, our ancestors were free to roam. They extended their range, bridging the gaps between water sources, crossing deserts and mountain barriers, meeting and mixing with others of their kind. The little pouches of liquid they carried were passports to new places, windows that opened on worlds that were once as remote to them as the stars.

It was a liberating experience, vividly recorded in images painted and engraved on every suitable surface. The water bearers were also picture makers, celebrating their conquests, capturing their prey over and over again in their minds, paying homage to the animals they ate. Shelters throughout Africa and Asia and southern Europe are festooned with lovely portraits of antelope and bison, wildebeest and woolly mammoth. And when one of these paleolithic artists finally had the leisure and the inclination to create the first known landscape, scratching the scene onto a piece of antler, the subject was not a mountain or the moon. It was a reindeer, shown just as it was always seen twenty-five thousand years ago beside a far more vital landmark—grazing in grass and sedge along the banks of a stream.

Composite: Petroglyphs, Valley of Fire, Nevada/ Hanakoa Falls, Kauai, Hawaii

Comanche Point and Colorado River, Grand Canyon, Arizona

Fisherman, Antigua, Lesser Antilles

The immersion continues. For all our independence, we remain bound to water sources as firmly as those ancestors who left their first stone tools in beds of river gravel. We may have stretched the connection, but we keep coming back to the well. Back to the margins of a world with which we have a deep affinity.

It is hard to put rivers out of our minds. They flow there, moving ceaselessly and yet remaining fixed, giving and taking life, potent symbols of our fate.

In a world prone to instability, rivers are comforting. They always move in the same direction. They are teachers of the elements of geography, reference points to which we can return. On the earliest known map—a plan of Babylonia carved into a four-thousand-year-old clay tablet—the Euphrates is the most obvious detail. The river is the center of the universe, bisecting the disk of the known world, a slash drawn through the heart of reality.

The sequence of rock art also makes it clear that people gradually turned from the rigors of the hunt to the subtle and more silent art of fishing.

Instead of following the herds, they went back to water for their protein and were able to enjoy a more truly settled existence, one that depended on a new skill and delicacy in toolmaking. On the manufacture of harpoons with barbed and detachable heads, and on the most sophisticated of all snares, the net. Proof of the success of these early techniques is that they are still practiced in much the same way today. We have better baits and hooks, and more mechanical methods of finding fish, but the practice itself remains largely unchanged. It is the only hunting and gathering activity that continues as an essential enterprise, even in our complex industrial society.

Fishing was also, right from the start, a spur to other things.

Sitting by the riverside, it cannot have been long before someone began, as fishermen will, to think of other things. To notice the quantities of flotsam passing by, and to wonder why some things float while others sink. To dream, in other words, of buoyancy.

Hance Rapids, Colorado River, Grand Canyon, Arizona

Rowboat, Spanish River, Ontario

Riverbanks have always been powerful influences over our lives, guiding and directing, sending travelers and their thoughts off at a tangent.

The waters are provocative, far from passive, offering an irresistible invitation to a free ride, either back to familiarity or on to the unknown. Rock engravings in the Algerian Sahara show hippo being hunted from reed boats when the desert was still a great lake, over six thousand years ago. The bones of deep-sea fish in middens on the Swedish coast suggest that craft of some kind, probably made of bark or skin, were being used there during the same period. All provide evidence of the same spirit of adventure, a curiosity born of a growing need to know where rivers go.

Rivercraft were the first of all vehicles. With them, areas that could be explored only by generations of effort became accessible to casual drift. Our ancestors paddled across water long before they learned to saddle a horse. They hoisted sail before they ever traveled on wheels along a road. It was simple rafts and dugouts that shrank the Stone Age, so that by the end of the last glaciation mounds of shells and fishbones had sprung up along shores all over the world, evidence of the rapid and waterborne spread of human habitation.

Sunset, Midway Lake, Alaska

Ever since the first humans put a stream between themselves and a sabre-toothed tiger, rivers have also assumed the function of defensive barriers. A river on one side of a camp was not only a source of food and drink, but a natural moat protecting that flank from attack.

Islands in larger rivers were even more easily defended, and it was not long before battlements grew up along streams and shores, elaborating and developing such natural fortifications. Invaders soon learned to use these barriers against their owners, diverting smaller rivers to leave defenders high and dry and deprived of their supplies. So, as early as five thousand years ago, people moved to take advantage of larger bodies of water. And all the lakes of Europe became studded with artificial islands of logs and mud, surmounted by stilted houses, which provided lake-dwellers with the sort of security only to be improved on very much later by the builders of great walls and military moats.

These people were the beneficiaries also of another aquatic insight.

Seeing a river do useful work, floating boats and bearing burdens, gave early hunters pause for thought. Twenty men might strain to move a boulder, shoving it laboriously along. But put it on the water, and a child can tow it away. So the rivers became slaves as well as teachers, freeing us from physical labor, making us inhumanly strong and giving us mastery over forces that once seemed beyond our control. And, in the process, opening up the possibility of other forms of domination over nature.

After we shifted part of our burden to water, other parts were delegated when we domesticated animals and plants.

The process began, perhaps ten thousand years ago, somewhere on the fertile plains of western Asia, in Mesopotamia—the land that lies in the midst of rivers, between the Tigris and the Euphrates. It was here, and along the Nile, the Indus, and the Hwang Ho, that early waterfront settlements prospered and grew, through domestication and skilled irrigation, into the great river civilizations.

163

Pointe Noire, Guadeloupe, Lesser Antilles

Santa Monica Mountains, California

The change began with modification of flint weapons into hoes and sickles, sparking the agricultural revolution. But it was the gathering of early cultivators and pastoralists along the banks of the older rivers that made the difference. The waters there were wide and slow, already half-tamed, prone to gentle annual overflow that automatically enriched the soils around them. And the muds and clays they left behind were easily worked, providing us with our first plastic, with a substance that would hold its shape, becoming a brick or a pot as it dried.

The collection and storage of a surplus of seasonal food shattered forever all natural limits to population size. Hunters and gatherers had to live only on what they could find. But people who could produce their own food, and plan and control its supply, were free to grow. Which they did, rapidly. And as communities grew, they became more complex.

Water created wealth. Land that had been improved by drainage or irrigation was now more desirable. And those who used and worked the best part grew more food and owned excess that gave them an advantage no nomad ever knew.

165

Mississippi River, St. Louis, Missouri

Inequities arose, dividing the world for the first time into rich and poor, making it necessary for the invention of specialists trained to defend those who had from those who were envious of them. Society fragmented into farmers and farm workers, soldiers and traders, potters, weavers, and smiths. And the diviners, those antlered shamans who once helped the hunters find their prey, became powerful priests, the first intelligentsia, keepers of the calendar and predictors of the season.

History is a watercourse. A river in the mind. A precarious pattern we make from the flow of time, as we try to write our names on the water.

Potters were the first to stem the flow, patting the riverbed into crude cups, coiling its clay into jars, spinning beautiful symmetries on their wheels. Coaxing the elements into submission, whipping them into shape, making something lasting out of water, mud, and sun.

Then came the priests, keeping track of the progress of the floods, noting the number of days that passed between one high water and another, averaging things out and looking to the stars for assistance. Making calendars, learning codes of writing, and taming time itself.

Civilization was born of settled agriculture out of marshy chaos, creating breeding grounds instead for new ideas. Towns grew into kingdoms or city states, and all this swift and heady evolution began with river control. There is a direct connection between the first mud huts on the Tigris and those marble monuments that later came to be reflected in the Tiber. Simple ditches grew into channels and sophisticated aquaducts, all leading from and to the river that was a prerequisite for such growth and lay at the heart of each society.

The splendor and glory of cities like Baghdad, which at its height had thirty thousand public baths, was not due to silk or gold but to the muddy rivers on which they lay.

The rulers of these great communities were first and foremost Lords of Water, judged by their ability to constrain the rivers and make these flow according to their will. They were river guardians, responsible for keeping up the waterworks, honored more for their engineering than their military skills. Legendary Menes, credited with the unification of Upper and Lower Egypt, is better known as the first to place a dam across the Nile.

Ohio-Erie Canal Restoration, Coshocton, Ohio

Centuries before Babylon subdued the warring city states, a series of waterways connected the Tigris and Euphrates, surrounding Sumer and Akkad with networks of canals. And it was to control the traffic in these, to collect the tolls, to administer and maintain the waterways, that bodies of rules and regulations were first drawn up. The Code of Hammurabi, the earliest and most influential model of community law, was concerned almost entirely with water rights.

As cities grew, they kept on tampering with their rivers, channeling and diverting, building bridges and tunnels, fighting drought with dams, doing the sort of cooperative work that only communities can. Exercising skills that brought together people of different interests and languages, extending professional and trading links up and down stream, opening their lives to exotic plants and alien ideas. Feeding an overflow that led inevitably to the formation of ancient empires that came to embrace the whole known civilized world.

167

Roosevelt Dam, Salt River Project, Arizona

Water barriers have been effective in keeping some people safe from untimely conquest. They protected the Japanese from the attentions of Kublai Khan; the English from the Armada, Napoleon, and even the Third Reich. But it is more generally true that rivers and seas have acted as highways, encouraging contact, fostering trade, and servicing the empires of Phoenicia, Venice, Portugal, and Britain.

Cyrus was the first great emperor, whose opening campaign against Babylon in 539 B.C. was delayed only by his fury with the river Gyndus for drowning one of his sacred white horses. He punished the mighty water by splitting it into 360 channels, each weak enough to be crossed "by a woman without wetting more than her knees."

He was of course a Persian, a newcomer, and therefore unfamiliar with the reverence due to rivers. People in the river civilizations treated them gently, approaching their banks with awe, making sacrifices appropriate to a god. But the conquerors were men of a different kind, less sympathetic to the sacred, more concerned with power than equilibrium.

And we, unfortunately, are their heirs.

We are the flood-tamers. Flushed with the success of technology, cutting, filling, diverting, blocking whole valleys with feats of extraordinary engineering. Damming rivers, turning them on or off at will, bringing deserts into bloom.

But we are also the flood-makers. Slashing, burning, felling the forests which once soaked up rain like gigantic green sponges. Nibbling away at the margins of nature, loosening absorbent soils and, during the last century alone, watching 25 percent of all arable land wash away into the sea.

We have added to earth's carbon dioxide concentration by our careless use of fossil fuels, turning the planet into a greenhouse warm enough to melt the ice caps, living on the ragged edge of demonstrating that what once happened to steamy Venus can happen here as well.

The problem is older than the Persian Empire. It begins with the exercise of the earliest water-linked skills.

The first machines were all instruments of irrigation. Devices like the Egyptian *shaduf,* consisting of a pole and a bucket and a counterpoise for lifting water. With it, a man was more than human, moving over a thousand gallons a day.

Hannibal Locks and Dam, Ohio River, Ohio

169

The first great civic works were aquaducts, amazing subterranean passages like the *kiraz* of Afghanistan, the *qanat* of Iran, and the *foggara* of Syria, which carried water for many miles from springs to fertile fields, making those who owned them independent of the seasons.

The first major superstructures, antedating even tombs, were all for storing water. Starting with earthworks in the Wadi Gerrawi on the eastern desert rim of Egypt; going on to the creation of Lake Homs in ancient Syria; through gravity dams on the Indus and in old Iran; to elegant stone constructions, complete with sluices, in China and in Greece. Through these, we learned to thumb our noses at the demons of drought.

But it was not until all such alienation was concentrated in one society that we came to hold nature at full arm's length.

It was the Romans who finally mastered all the water arts, building their great empire, not so much to the glory of the gods as in gratitude to good plumbing. They drained swamps and irrigated deserts, pumping in water and piping out sewage everywhere they traveled. It was their roads, their dams and drains, their bridges, fountains, and conduits, that survived right through the Dark Ages to provide the foundations for the Industrial Revolution.

Ohio River at Belmont, West Virginia

Pollution, Allegan County, Michigan

All the great cities of the modern world have grown up on waterfronts. Industry demands it. Where people need only 10 pounds of water to supply each pound of flesh, it takes 250 pounds of water to make a pound of paper, and 600 to produce the one pound of fertilizer.

In the United States alone, industry uses over one hundred cubic miles of water every year to cool, wash, and circulate its materials. That is 30 percent of all the water in the rivers of the world. And very little of it goes back cleaner than it came out.

Pollution is relative and hard to define. Floods and dead hippos are polluters, but their effects are local and tend to be temporary. Pollution problems today are most often the result of pesticides or fertilizers used in agriculture, of the wastes produced directly by farm animals, of careless disposal of sewage, of an accumulation of domestic refuse and synthetic detergent, and of oil spills, and the toxic discharge of industrial effluent. There are chemical, physical, and thermal pollutants—and increasing concerns about radioactive wastes. Nuclear power stations are all water-cooled and inordinately thirsty. Those of France alone already use more water than can be provided by the total surface runoff in that nation.

This is becoming a common problem. Water consumption in many countries now exceeds the natural supply, and budgets can only be balanced by processing and recycling what there is. Every city dweller makes direct use of between 100 and 150 gallons a day, 80 percent of which returns, contaminated in some way, to the city's sewers and flows back into river, lake, or sea. In more efficient cities, much of this waste is recovered, filtered, and treated, usually with one part per million of chlorine, and used again. But many cities remain profligate, not only wasteful, but mindless of those downstream. It is hard for people in arid areas to have much sympathy with New York, for instance, when its residents complain of water shortages while billions of gallons flow past them, polluted, to the sea.

Expectations of water purity differ, but perhaps the best and least emotive measure of pollution is that used in Britain. A healthy fish is placed in the water there, and if it dies, the source is polluted and must be purified. Where arguments arise and comparisons need to be made, the degree of pollution is calculated as one hundred divided by the survival time in minutes.

It is significant, perhaps, that action against pollution in most countries has been taken, not as a result of complaints by those who drink the water, but in deference to protests from line-fishing members of the electorate. Those who get closest to the source in its raw state. Agitation by fishermen against the toxic condition of the Thames two decades ago led to a clean-up campaign that has seen the recent return of several species of fish, including the sensitive salmon.

Water is a valuable raw material. It is heavy and expensive to move. The largest tanker ever built can hold only about a thousand dollars' worth. But water, nevertheless, remains astonishingly cheap. A gallon of wine costs as much as ten gallons of milk or twenty gallons of petroleum. But for the same price, in most countries, you can still get one hundred thousand gallons of water.

Fisherman, North Channel Islands, Lake Huron, Ontario

The secret lies in the quantities used. Almost two thousand gallons a day are required to house, clothe, feed, and move every American citizen, making the capital costs for water development in the United States comparable to most other kinds of investment. In countries with less generous water resources, unit costs are naturally higher. High enough, in some instances, to make it worthwhile to think about towing icebergs up from the Antarctic and letting them melt off desert shores. An ice cube just a mile across would provide one trillion gallons of fresh water, enough to meet the needs of the entire population of Kuwait for a year.

Beached Icebergs, Lamplugh Glacier, Glacier Bay, Alaska

Moses once solved another desert thirst by striking the rock of Horeb with his staff. Others since have used a variety of such divining rods to locate buried sources, responding to a sensitivity all life seems to share for the presence of water nearby. Because fresh water is less dense than salt, a lens of it floats just beneath the surface of the sand on most coral shores, and is easily reached; but inland, it is necessary to dig a good deal deeper.

There are ancient wells in Iran and Oman that go down several hundred feet, but it was not until the invention of the rotary drill that we were able to take advantage of extensive reservoirs as much as four and five miles underground.

We can go on mining and moving water for a while yet. Estimates suggest that we will reach our natural water limits only in another century, when earth's present population has quadrupled. But sooner or later, we are going to have to think about drinking the sea.

It already makes economic sense in some areas. A total of over a billion gallons a day is being produced now by desalination. This involves either distillation, taking water out of the salt, or reverse osmosis, taking salt out of the water. Both processes are proving effective and, for the first time ever, a river of fresh water is flowing out of, instead of into, the sea.

Such techniques may help us come to terms with the need to cherish and conserve our most valuable resource. It is worth bearing in mind that it is not unlimited, and that we already use two hundred times more water by weight than any other material in our lives.

A lot of it still goes to agriculture, which remains totally water-dependent.

The richest, best-fed countries are always those with reliable water supplies. Today this means those in temperate zones with enough rain to guarantee regular crops. Arid and semiarid zones tend to live permanently on the edge of famine. It is this threat that forces half a billion people out onto tropical floodplains, where they borrow land from moody rivers to grow the crops that feed one-third of the world. And by doing so, they put their own lives at risk, because sooner or later these rivers come back to claim their own.

Dawn, La Désirade, Lesser Antilles

Sugar Cane, Oak Alley Plantation, Louisiana

Cultivation of any kind represents a threat to earth's ecology. It usually means a monoculture of some sort, a concentration of just one kind of plant, which uses far more water than any natural ecosystem. Citrus, cotton, and sugarcane, for instance, are notoriously thirsty, using up to ten thousand pounds of water to produce each pound of crop.

Agriculture also involves, more often than not, the introduction of plants that do not belong. Australian eucalyptuses, for example, are popular everywhere because they grow rapidly in any reasonably warm climate. But they are so water-hungry that their requirements nearly always exceed the local supply. They have been used deliberately to dry up unwanted swamps in North Africa, but in most places their careless cultivation has begun to create havoc. These and other species are changing the levels of water tables, altering flow in natural channels, interfering with normal drainage patterns and making floods, when these do occur, far more devastating.

The agricultural revolution changed both our lives and our minds.

Nomads can simply follow their herds, traveling to where the rains have fallen. But farmers are tied to the land, leaving them inherently insecure, prepared to try anything to satisfy their thirsts.

Religion is one of the results. Right from the very beginning, gods have tended to reflect the concerns of their people. So it comes as no surprise to discover that all the earliest deities who had a fixed abode were Water Lords.

In Assyro-Babylonian myth, water is the primordial element and comes from Apsu, an abyss which encircles the earth and is personified as Enki or Ea, begetter of springs and rivers, father of Nanshe, the goddess of canals.

For the Chaldeans and Persians, it was Anahita; for the Egyptians, Canopus; for the Indians, the goddess Apa; and for the Phoenicians, Aleyin—"he who rides the clouds." In ancient Chinese ritual, it is Shui-kuan—the Agent of Water, who averts evil from heaven and earth. The Incan creator is bearded Viracocha, "the foam on Lake Titicaca," who emerges from the water to make the sun, the moon, and the stars. And the Greek panoply begins with great Oceanus, the river that girdles the universe; and devolves through a heirarchy of Titans such as Tethys, who gave birth to three thousand rivers, on to the Olympians under Poseidon.

179

Isle of Rhum, Sea of the Inner Hebrides, Scotland

In the beginning, there was only water. For the Mayans, a peaceful sea under a vast emptiness of sky, waiting to be disturbed by the storm god Huracan. For Pima and Apache, Chuckchi and Blackfoot, nothing moves until Old Man comes floating by on his raft, willing the world into existence. Commanding, like Yaweh of the Hebrews, that there be a firmament in the midst of the waters. From then on, it is up to Finnish Ahto, Babylonian Tiamat, or Roman Maia to keep the land well watered, giving sustenance to the people and their crops. And it is the duty of all priests to act as go-betweens, urging such deities to intercede on our behalf.

Rainmakers in New Guinea prime the pumps by sprinkling water from a dripping bough. The Omaha and Natchez spit it out in a provocative spray. The Angoni and Baronga in Africa rely on ribald songs, preferably performed by twins. In the Caucasus, girls yoke themselves to a plough and drag it into a dry riverbed. In Transylvania, they sit naked on a harrow. The Arunta in Australia construct votive rainbows over a dead snake. In Madras, women of the appropriate caste catch a live frog and tie it to a fan. The details differ, but everywhere the purpose is the same, to catch and hold the attention of the gods, to invoke their pity with prayer and procession—and to keep the water flowing.

Water is the oldest archetype. A power for good and evil. A life-giving force, but one capable of becoming a destructive flood or tidal wave.

This dual nature invests all moving water with edgy spirits, which range from horse-legged, fish-tailed Tritons to seductive Sirens. The myths of every nation are replete with Old Men of the Sea, puzzling and unpredictable characters much given to shape-shifting and sooth-saying. And with undines and nixies, women with long tresses who tend to sit on riverbanks, waiting for unwary youths to captivate and drown.

181

White Peak, Derbyshire, England

Littlefield Fountain, The University of Texas at Austin, Texas

A few water-beings, Neptune and his lascivious horde, Proteus and the Nereids, have become marine. But all are originally freshwater deities, guardians and guarantors of the water we need. Expression of our ambivalence toward all the powers of nature, which both give and take away.

Still waters are usually seen as more benign. The wells and pools and fountains of the world are places of solace and veneration, inhabited by gentle nymphs and water maidens. The homes of Naiads, Potamids, and Crenae; who are essentially benevolent, weaving and spinning, blessed with the gift of prophecy, which can be purchased by the offering of a needle or a coin. Hence the many wishing wells. All places of pilgrimage and worship, paved with special stone, adorned by a sacred rock or carving, surrounded by plants with magical properties. They have their own power as well as a special melancholy, and most stand today at the heart of a shrine or parish, or mark the boundary of tribal territories and medieval counties.

Zilker Gardens, Austin, Texas

Rhiwnant, Elan Valley, Wales

Some waters were always seen to be more beneficial than others.

Every folklore has its Fountain of Youth or its Well of Knowledge. The healing pool of Bethesda in Jerusalem, the Great Saliva Lake of the Tang Emperors, the Moon Washing Spring in Japan. Places for taking the water cure. The Holy Sepulchre in early Christian liturgy is described as the fountain of life and resurrection. When Quetzalcoatl sails out to sea on a raft of snakes, he heads for the country of the sun, where he finds and drinks the Water of Immortality. Slavic tales tell of *shivaya voda*, the water capable even of bringing the dead back to life.

And all water, everywhere, cleanses and absolves, purifying both body and soul.

Water, in most cultures, is taken as a sign of grace and used to mark fresh starts, naming ceremonies, and initiations. Christian baptism, which ranges from total immersion to the token sprinkling of an infant, has its roots in Confucian custom, in the Hindu practice of bathing in the Ganges, in the Greek idea of cartharsis, and in rituals refined by the Nile-conscious Egyptians. And holy water has its secular counterpart in symbolic acts practiced publicly by men such as Pontius Pilate and, more privately, by Jaggers, the lawyer, in Dickens' *Great Expectations*, who ends each court case in a closet, washing the latest client from his hands.

Gordale Scar, North Yorkshire, England

Red Deer, Kilmory, Isle of Rhum, Scotland

The greatest ablution of all, of course, was The Flood, the deluge that is said at one time to have covered most of earth.

There are tales of inundation from India, China, South America, and Polynesia. From Genesis to the Epic of Gilgamesh. Accounts of wickedness wiped out and the salvation of a favored few in the arks of Noah, Tezpi, or Utnapishtim. There is a haunting similarity in these stories, with their poetic messages of deep, stormy waters and the rainbowed promises. All tell of incessant rain or sudden tidal wave, of the release of a symbolic bird which returns with fresh vegetation, and of new beginnings on an isolated mountain.

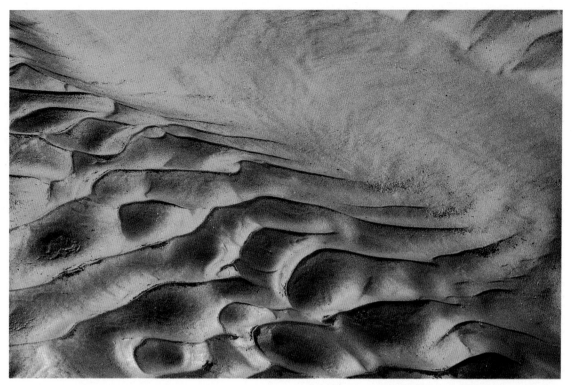

Low Water, Colorado River, Grand Canyon, Arizona

There is some support for these allegories in modern archaeology.

Assyrian tablets from the library of Ashurbanipal tell of survivors rescued from a flood in a great boat built by a priestly king. Excavations at Ur of the Chaldees reveal a record of the growth of civilization, broken only by a ten-foot layer of silt in which there are no remains of human life. The Asian sequence is interrupted by several such massive overflows, the first recorded in 2297 B.C., earning the Hwang Ho its alternative name of "China's Sorrow."

Bore holes sunk for oil in Iraq and in the Gulf of Mexico pass through thick alluvial clay, with an antediluvian layer of freshwater shells at its base. And there is a distinctive band of fine mud, an indication of unusually heavy river flow, in cores taken from all over the eastern Mediterranean. Geologists everywhere find evidence of catastrophe and sudden inundation; some, but not all of it, caused by a great melt at the end of the last ice age.

Earth, it seems, is naturally prone to periodic flooding. It is how things here are, and none of it was a disaster until humans arrived on the scene, coloring circumstance with our desires and our dreams.

We have moist imaginations. In them, water is the eye of the earth. A bright eye which in clear pools becomes a mirror, letting us see our own reflections, making each of us the center of a world. In deeper pools, it darkens and becomes somber and unfathomable, hinting instead of drowning and death by flood.

When water is disturbed, it is ambivalent, provocative. With moods that mirror ours, ranting from ripples of interest and awareness, to the savage seas of rage and fury. And through all these manifestations, it carries a maternal voice and reminders of the womb.

Water is essentially feminine, a mother figure. All our best-loved heroes emerge from it as though they came from the uterus of earth. Their parents are usually nameless and they rise from river or sea like the sun, representing humanity at large.

Sargon, the founder of Babylon, is rescued from the reeds by Akki, "the water-carrier." Karna, the focus of an ancient Indian epic, is discovered floating on the Ganges. Each is abandoned, exposed, as Noah and his family are, to the hazards of flood. The ark is even described in the Old Testament by the same word, *tebah*, as that used for the basket in which Moses, whose name means "the water-drawer," is found on the Nile.

There is a close association in our minds between water and babies. We bear both and give foundlings over to the care of a "wet" nurse. The Dagomba in Africa believe that a dream of one's wife carrying water is a prophecy of pregnancy. And Freud has no hesitation in interpreting dreams of water as memories of being born. Reflections, in fact. Which is why ceremonies of immersion and baptism are so easily and widely understood as metaphors for being born again.

Silver Grotto, Shinumo Wash, Grand Canyon, Arizona

Dawn Mist, Lakeville, Connecticut

The same symbolism is evident in art, where water is seldom what it seems.

Christian painting abounds in religious references.

Christ transcends by walking on the water, or stands on a mound from which flow four streams representing the gospels or the rivers that encompass the Garden of Eden. Pontius Pilate strives for absolution and John the Baptist for redemption through the waters of innocence. The water of the Eucharist stands for humanity in contrast to the wine of divinity. A fountain is an attribute of the Virgin Mary, the source of living water.

Change in classic hands is signaled by the river that Hercules diverts through the Augean stables; transition by the ferryman Charon going about his business on the Styx; and vulnerability by the immersion of all but the critical heel of Achilles beneath the same dark waters. Later painters are more impressionistic, content to let Ophelia and her floating tresses speak of the end of youth and spring, or groups of bathers provide a gentle allegory of life at its height in summer.

The psychological contrast between water and land has also been employed to great effect in architecture.

The best seaside towns all face their horizons, emphasizing the fact that they stand on the edge of the deep. The most satisfying waterfront properties lean out right over lake or harbor, giving an even greater sense of this immediacy. The most harmonious cities are those whose buildings can be reflected in a river that flows easily between them, going about its business as a vital artery in urban metabolism. It is no accident that Venice has the power to move most imaginations.

Industrial Site along the Ohio River, West Virginia

Even where the water is not functional, as in ornamental fountains and pools, its presence serves to enhance architectural composition. It organizes space, opening areas up as do mirrors in a room, creating continuity and providing both physical and spiritual relief. There is something about almost any body of water that fascinates us, attracting courting couples and our coins like a magnet.

The aesthetic appeal has something to do, perhaps, with the way in which water can help us relate to the natural world. It is the source of all things and continues to symbolize fertility and purity, birth and death, time and timelessness, smoothing out rough edges in the complex geometry of our lives.

Water, in addition, has a very distinctive voice. A liquid language which ranges from the bantering jargon of the brook, to the full-blown tirade of a sea in storm. And all these sounds find sympathetic expression in the tone poetry of music.

Felix Mendelssohn was among the first and most accomplished composers of what came to be known as program music. He studied painting, and his orchestral seascapes are the direct equivalent in music of the marine pictures being produced in the early nineteenth century by his contemporary Joseph Turner. *Becalmed at Sea* is an unmistakable rendering of the threatening nature of an ocean unnaturally still. And his Hebridean overture contains the best of all musical impressions of stormy waters, as he saw them at the awesome mouth of *Fingal's Cave*.

The *Ocean Symphony* of Nicholas Rubinstein is sound painting on an even richer, grander scale. But it was Claude Debussy who took the fluid art of music totally beyond the static confines of the canvas with his symphonic sketches for *La Mer*, in which he successfully portrayed the sea, a world of wind and wave, light and spray, in all its changing moods. And this poetic process was completed in more modern vein by Vaughan Williams' *Sea Symphony*.

193

Seascape, Na Pali Coast, Kauai, Hawaii

Upper Carbet Falls, La Soufrière, Guadeloupe, Lesser Antilles

Musical landscapes of fresh water are less obvious.

They begin with Bavarian yodels imitating waterfalls and progress through Mendelssohn's piano pieces such as *The Rivulet,* to the *Rain Sonata* of Johannes Brahms, in which the piano part follows an incessant running figure that suggests the gentle pattern of a shower. Franz Schubert's water songs, Franz Listz's *Au bord d'une source,* and Maurice Ravel's *Jeux d'eau* take the process a stage further by creating an interplay of both words and music, in which rippling arpeggios and running passages are, together, something distinctively liquid.

Music that does not pretend to portray, but was clearly inspired by, water must include Frederic Chopin's gloomy prelude known as *The Raindrop,* which was written under the leaky roof of a monastery in Majorca during the terrible winter of 1838. And perhaps Luigi Cherubini's grand opera *The Water Carrier.*

Caribbean Sea, Cupecoy Beach, Saint Martin, Lesser Antilles

Lower Falls of the Yellowstone River, Wyoming

George Frideric Handel's celebrated *Water Music*, which is reputed to have been written to appease King George I and played on the Thames by musicians in hot pursuit of the royal barge, may not have any true aquatic connections at all. But there is a whole body of music directly inspired by a more modern water sport. Between 1961 and 1965, thousands of recordings of surf music poured out of southern California. Heavy in reverberation and light on intellect, these simple odes to waves, girls, and cars are best represented by the fluid harmonies of the Beach Boys.

Water is liquid imagination, the nearest we can get to a materialization of mind. And reflection, the mind's ability to think deeply about anything, is a natural water term. So, it is in the reflection of poetic minds that we come closest to touching and understanding water's soul.

Each culture attaches its own symbolic framework to the forms in which water appears, but there are underlying themes in all water imagery which seem to be universal and revealing.

Mooney Falls, Havasu Creek, Arizona

Little Colorado River Gorge at Hopi Salt Canyon, Arizona

Water is deep. It holds shadows and darker shades, and is linked with sleep, the unconscious, and death. To look into it too long is to court the fate of Narcissus. Edgar Allan Poe's inspirations abound in such heavy water imagery, in which "the lily lolls upon the wave" and dark rivers flow through "the meadows of sorrow."

Water is pure. It wets and washes everything, renewing and reviving, making it possible for us to be born again. It is crystal, clear, limpid, the "adorner and refresher of the world." It is something holy, performing, in the words of John Keats, a "priestlike task of pure ablution round earth's human shores."

Water is fresh. It serves us directly, soothing, cooling, and quenching our thirst. It is the source of peace and reveries, something sweet and gentle, designed to ease our pain. The presence of salt in it is a perversion, the stuff of nightmares like those of Samuel Taylor Coleridge, who found "Water, water, everywhere, nor any drop to drink."

Water is alluring. It drags people down to the shore. It sends young men to sea. You can watch it for hours, it goes on and on, exerting an attraction like no other substance. "Were Niagara but a cataract of sand," asks Herman Melville, "would you travel your thousand miles to see it?"

Probably not. And that, perhaps, is water's real attraction. It is ungraspable, a very lively phantom.

It moves, like blood or milk, washing to and fro in the womb. Passing, in Percy Bysshe Shelley's image, "through the pores of the ocean and shores," changing, but never dying. It is T. S. Eliot's "strong brown god—sullen, untamed and intractable—keeping his seasons and rages, destroyer, reminder of what men choose to forget."

It is all these things and many, many more.

Water meanders. It is hard to pin down, but five centuries ago a great and very liquid intelligence came close to obtaining a submission.

"Water," said Leonardo da Vinci, "is sometimes sharp and sometimes strong, sometimes acid and sometimes bitter, sometimes sweet and sometimes thick or thin, sometimes it is seen bringing hurt or pestilence, sometimes health-giving, sometimes poisonous. It suffers change into as many natures as are the different places through which it passes. And as the mirror changes with the color of its object, so it alters with the nature of the place, becoming: noisome, laxative, astringent, sulfurous, salt, incarnadined, mournful, raging, angry, red, yellow, green, black, blue, greasy, fat or slim. Sometimes it starts a conflagration, sometimes it extinguishes one; is warm and is cold, carries away or sets down, hollows out or builds up, tears down or establishes, fills or empties, raises itself or burrows down, speeds or is still; is the cause at times of life or death, or increase or privation, nourishes at times and at others does the contrary; at times has a tang, at times it is without savor, sometimes submerging the valleys with great floods. In time and with water, everything changes."

Just so.

Kalalau Sunset, Na Pali Coast, Kauai, Hawaii

FURTHER READING

Alexandersson, O. *Living Water*. Turnstone: Northampshire, 1982.

Bachelard, G. *Water and Dreams*. Pegasus Foundation: Dallas, 1983.

Bardach, J. *Downstream*. Harper & Row: New York, 1964.

Briggs, P. *Water—the Vital Essence*. Harper & Row: New York, 1967.

Brittain, R. E. *Rivers, Man and Myths*. Doubleday: New York, 1967.

Chorley, R. J. (ed.) *Water, Earth and Man*. Methuen: London, 1969.

Claiborne, R. *Climate, Man and History*. W. W. Norton: New York, 1970.

Cocannouer, J. A. *Water—and the Cycle of Life*. Devin-Adair: New York, 1958.

Collis, J. S. *The Moving Waters*. William Sloane: New York, 1955.

Davis, K. S. *Water—the Mirror of Science*. Anchor/ Doubleday: New York, 1961.

Errington, P. L. *Of Men and Marshes*. Iowa State University Press: Ames, 1957.

Forman, J. (ed.) *Water and Man*. Friends of the Land: Columbus, Ohio, 1950.

Fox, C. S. *Water*. Technical Press: Kingston Hill, Surrey, 1951.

Franks, F. (ed.) *Water—a Comprehensive Treatise*. Plenum: New York, 1972.

Furon, R. *The Problem of Water*. Elsevier: New York, 1963.

Gerhardt, M. I. *Old Men of the Sea*. Polak and Van Gennep: Amsterdam, 1967.

Hope, R. C. *The Legendary Lore of the Holy Wells of England*. Elliot Stock: London, 1893.

Hunt, C. A. and Garrels, R. M. *Water—the Web of Life*. W. W. Norton: New York, 1972.

King, T. *Water—Miracle of Nature*. Macmillan: New York, 1953.

Kuenen, P. H. *Realms of Water*. John Wiley: New York, 1955.

Leopold, L. B. and Davis, K. S. *Water*. Time-Life International: Netherlands, 1968.

Litton, R. B. et al. *Water and Landscape*. Water Information Centre: New York, 1974.

Milne, A. *Floodshock*. Alan Sutton: Gloucester, 1986.

Milne, L. and Milne, M. *Water and Life*. Andre Deutsch: London, 1965.

Morgan, E. *The Aquatic Ape*. Souvenir: London, 1982.

Olson, R. E. *A Geography of Water*. William Brown: Dubuque, Iowa, 1970.

Platt, R. H. *Water—the Wonder of Life*. Prentice-Hall: Englewood Cliffs, New Jersey, 1971.

Petts, G. E. *Rivers*. Butterworths: London, 1983.

Raikes, R. *Water, Weather and Prehistory*. John Baker: London, 1967.

Schwenk, T. *Sensitive Chaos*. Schocken: New York, 1976.

Walton, W. C. *The World of Water*. Taplinger: New York, 1970.

Watson, L. *Dreams of Dragons*. William Morrow: New York, 1986.

Wendt, H. *The Romance of Water*. Hill and Wang: New York, 1983.

INDEX